Beyond Practical Virtue

Beyond Practical Virtue

A Defense of Liberal Democracy through Literature

JOEL A. JOHNSON

University of Missouri Press
Columbia and London

Library of Congress Cataloging-in-Publication Data

Johnson, Joel A., 1974–
    Beyond practical virtue : a defense of liberal democracy through literature /
Joel A. Johnson.
        p. cm.
    Summary: "Johnson examines the worth of liberal democracy and the question of
cultural development by looking at novels by James Fenimore Cooper, Mark Twain, and
William Dean Howells. Using the fictions to explore the richness of everyday life, he
offers new insight into the relationship between the state and the individual"—Provided
by publisher.
    Includes bibliographical references and index.
    ISBN 978-0-8262-1711-0 (alk. paper)
    1. American fiction—19th century—History and criticism.   2. Liberalism in
literature.   3. Democracy in literature.   4. Individualism in literature.   5. Liberalism.
6. Democracy.   7. Individualism.   8. Cooper, James Fenimore, 1789–1851—Criticism
and interpretation.   9. Twain, Mark, 1835–1910—Criticism and interpretation.
10. Howells, William Dean, 1837–1920—Criticism and interpretation.   I. Title.

    PS374.L42J65 2007
    813'.409358—dc22

                                                                        2007002485

DESIGNER: KRISTIE LEE
TYPESETTER: THE COMPOSING ROOM OF MICHIGAN, INC.
PRINTER AND BINDER: THE MAPLE-VAIL BOOK MANUFACTURING GROUP
TYPEFACES: ADOBE GARAMOND AND OPTIMA

For Diedre

"To get the full value of a joy you must have somebody to divide it with." —Mark Twain, *Following the Equator*

Contents

Preface

THESE ARE TROUBLING TIMES for democracy. Every day, newspaper headlines make clear the many ways in which the spread of democracy—once considered inevitable—has become severely constrained. Under U.S. guidance, Iraq has made only the first, halting steps toward stable popular rule, while Iran seems willing to challenge Western civilization to a nuclear showdown. Russia is still far from being a reliable democracy, and China continues its spectacular accession to global power, all without a speck of political liberalization. For the most part, Europe finds itself paralyzed into inaction, no longer capable of effectively motivating global democratization. Meanwhile, petty authoritarians in countries like Venezuela, taking advantage of America's insatiable demand for energy, are busy consolidating their power.

Faced with radical Islam's confidence and the setbacks democracy has experienced of late, Americans and other friends of democracy have tended to lose faith. Can democracy really be the best form of government, we ask ourselves secretly, if so many of those who reject democracy are willing to die in order to destroy it? Could it be that they see serious flaws in our beloved regime that we either have not seen or have chosen to ignore?

We tend to answer these questions in absolute terms: either we ourselves are to blame for hastily pushing a deeply flawed regime on the rest of the world, or the rest of the world is simply crazy for not adopting democracy—which is *obviously* the best regime the world has known. As with most controversial questions, the truth is likely not at either extreme. However, it is emotionally and cognitively difficult to maintain a middling position regarding modern democracy and its opponents, given the need to examine critically both one's own views (as knee-jerk patriots forget to do) and the views of democracy's opponents (which cultural relativists refuse to do).

In this state of affairs, we would be wise to revisit a critique that has been nipping at democracy's heels since at least the nineteenth century: a critique that was safely ignored so long as democracy was confidently striding forward, using its overwhelming economic and military might to level all obstacles in its way. Now that the world's ardor for democracy has cooled, it makes sense to look back at this critique, to see if we can better understand why democracy has ground to a stall. Perhaps, in the exuberance of youth, democracy and its supporters could ignore how democracy seems to give rise to an amoral, conformist culture where all freely chosen ends are considered equally legitimate. It is now time, however, for a more mature and sober assessment of democracy's strengths and weaknesses.

In this book, I engage the trenchant but often-ignored aesthetic critique of democracy, which posits that the conditions of liberty and equality level out life in such a way that every citizen in a democracy comes to possess nothing less than, but also nothing more than, a mediocre soul. In taking this critique seriously, I feel as if I am rifling through the private correspondence of a favorite deceased aunt, whose letters reveal a dark side not publicly evident during her exuberant life. Fortunately, democracy is not dead—nor is it likely to be so anytime soon. However, it is no longer in the blossom of youth, and we would be wise to know thoroughly its true character. We must know what its chief virtues and chief vices are, the latter of which are often not apparent. Perhaps, by looking back to the aesthetic critique, we can better understand democracy's current difficulties in appealing to the world, and think more productively about how democracy can better address the needs of the whole person.

Although my subject is individual development, this book is hardly an individual's accomplishment. Had I not received valuable support and guidance throughout the writing process, the result would have been far less satisfactory.

This project has distant origins in my Harvard University dissertation, which benefited from the tough-minded but sympathetic criticisms of an extraordinary quartet of advisers. Russell Muirhead saw where I was going before I did, and he masterfully conducted me through the process of developing an interesting topic. Richard Tuck, with his amazing knowledge of the history of political thought, was especially helpful in my coming to grips with the aesthetic critique. Philip Fisher kindly overlooked the crudeness of my attempts at literary analysis. Finally, and most importantly, Michael Sandel executed the office of committee chair with wisdom and enthusiasm. His suggestions for framing my arguments substantially improved the work as a whole. With the support of Michael and Glyn Morgan, I received a Core Fellowship to continue research for a year at Harvard after completing my Ph.D.

As the manuscript developed over the years, many others offered their reflections. My mother, Beth Johnson—a true book lover—has always been my most careful reader. By now, she probably knows this text better than I do. My father, Mark Johnson, has offered numerous insights from his areas of expertise: science and religion. Without my parents' support and encouragement, none of this would have been possible. Greg Kaster, in addition to being the most powerful positive influence on my writing style, read drafts of several chapters and provided many helpful recommendations. Philip Abbott and Robert Martin critiqued an early expression of my ideas at an annual meeting of the American Political Science Association. Participants in Harvard's Political Theory Research Colloquium, the Faculty Research Colloquium at Augustana College, and the Government Club at Augustana College have all given interesting and useful feedback at various stages of the manuscript's development. My students at Harvard and Augustana, particularly those in my politics and literature classes, have continued to inspire my research. Finally, I am grateful to be teaching in a wonderfully supportive and intellectually engaged department with Peter Schotten, Joe Dondelinger, and Brent Lerseth.

The editorial staff at the University of Missouri Press have been instrumental in making this book reach its potential. I am particularly indebted to Gary Kass for his tireless work in behalf of the manuscript. Thanks also to the anonymous reviewers for the press, who offered incisive recommendations for revision; and to Gloria Thomas Beckfield, whose wonderful copyediting assistance ensured that my words would speak my mind.

It goes without saying that, although this book is far better as a result of all the helpful criticism it has received, any flaws that remain are my responsibility alone.

My only regret is that the man who first introduced me to the study of political philosophy, Ron Christensen, did not live to see the completion of this project. His memory has been an inspiration throughout my years of studying politics.

My sons, Aaron and Alexander, remind me daily of the joys of discovery and the importance of play. My deepest thanks, though, go to my wife, Diedre, whose unwavering support, astounding patience, and cheerful spirit have sustained me through college, graduate school, fatherhood, and the life of a professor. In recognition, I dedicate this work to her.

Abbreviations

FOR THE SAKE OF convenience, the following abbreviated citations for the novels under discussion are embedded in the text.

James Fenimore Cooper
(Volume references are from *Works of J. Fenimore Cooper.*)
CB   *The Chainbearer* (vol. 6)
DS   *The Deerslayer* (vol. 1)
LM   *The Last of the Mohicans* (vol. 2)
HB   *Homeward Bound* (vol. 5)
P   *The Pioneers* (vol. 1)
ST   *Satanstoe* (vol. 8)

Mark Twain
CY   *A Connecticut Yankee in King Arthur's Court*
HF   *Adventures of Huckleberry Finn*

William Dean Howells
HNF   *A Hazard of New Fortunes*
SL   *The Rise of Silas Lapham*

Beyond Practical Virtue

Introduction

ADVANCES IN TECHNOLOGY and communications, combined with unparalleled prosperity, have given Western liberal democracies—in particular the United States—a unique ability to transmit their values far and wide. Most Americans exude confidence about democracy's attractiveness as a regime. After all, what rational person would choose authoritarian oppression over freedom, equality, and prosperity? As David Rothkopf puts it, "The United States should not hesitate to promote its values. In an effort to be polite or politic, Americans should not deny the fact that of all the nations in the history of the world, theirs is the most just, the most tolerant, the most willing to constantly reassess and improve itself, and the best model for the future."[1]

But is liberal democracy really "the best model for the future"? Developing nations have been reluctant to adopt liberal democratic institutions, and resistance to U.S. influence has been mounting. The tragic events of September 11, 2001, made it brutally clear that liberal democracy's global ascendancy is hardly inevitable. We must be prepared, therefore, to offer a full justification of liberal democracy, one that not only addresses current criticisms, but anticipates future objections.

The tensions arising from the spread of liberal democracy have already led to modifications in liberal theory. It is no longer sufficient, for example, to laud the benefits of equal rights, when the exercise of those rights can result in enormous material inequality; or to glorify free elections,

---

1. David Rothkopf, "In Praise of Cultural Imperialism?" 48–49.

which often merely legitimize the rule of an oligarchy. Progressive democrats have sought to address these problems by advocating a Third Way in domestic economic policy, offering tangible assistance to democratizing nations and advancing humbler theories of liberal democracy (such as John Rawls's political theory of justice[2]).

Where liberal theorists have been less successful, however, is in dealing with liberalism's effects on culture. Civic republicans, for example, have criticized liberals for refusing to use state power to instill citizens with virtue. Liberal neutrality, republicans argue, precludes the sort of civic education necessary for self-government.[3] A second culture-based argument, favored by antiglobalization activists, is that liberalism's universalistic claims tend to undermine traditional ways of life. Though liberalism appears tolerant, it nonetheless privileges those customs and practices that derive from free choice and can be justified with reference to human rights and other universal standards. All other traditions are left to wither away. As Pat Buchanan puts it, the losers in a globalized system of free trade are "the rooted people, the conservative people tied by the bonds of family, memory, and neighborhood to one community and one country."[4]

It is not my purpose to reply to these criticisms, about which much has already been written. Instead, I shall call attention to a third cultural issue that liberals have inadequately addressed: whether people tend to develop fully as individuals under liberal democracy. In other words, are citizens able to realize their own individual talents and capacities, despite living under a regime that does little formally to encourage such development? A full justification of liberal democracy must include a discussion of this problem, just as it must address questions of civic virtue and economic prosperity. The question of cultural development is a thorny one, given the number of brutal twentieth-century attempts to bring about cultural "improvement" through state action. It is understandable, then, that modern liberals primarily concern themselves with determining the nature and extent of individual and communal rights vis-à-vis society and with estab-

2. John Rawls, *Political Liberalism,* 9–11.

3. See, for example, Michael J. Sandel, *Democracy's Discontent,* and George F. Will, *Statecraft as Soulcraft.*

4. Patrick J. Buchanan, *The Great Betrayal,* 57. See also the antiglobalization essays collected in Jerry Mander and Edward Goldsmith, eds., *The Case against the Global Economy.*

lishing the sorts of civic virtues necessary for sustaining those rights. Even those liberals, such as Joseph Raz, who recognize a need for moderate amounts of state paternalism dramatically restrict the means available to the state for pursuing moral ideals.[5]

Although the liberal fear of state-guided cultural development is well founded, it should not prevent us from evaluating liberalism's effect on individual flourishing. We need an accurate accounting of the costs associated with our regime (what we must sacrifice to have peace, prosperity, and justice) so that our justification of liberalism can be balanced and honest. Maybe it *is* impossible to have both liberal democracy and a high degree of individual development, but we can hardly draw that conclusion without a thorough investigation.

In this book I examine and respond to a critique of liberal democracy espoused by such nineteenth- and twentieth-century writers as Thomas Carlyle, Friedrich Nietzsche, and T. S. Eliot. In its essentials, it is an aesthetic critique primarily concerned with how liberal democratic institutions impoverish citizens' souls by stripping society of all elevating and enlightening influences. Rather than encouraging individual development, the critics argue, modern democracy tends to stifle people into mediocrity. The critics consider liberal democracy and individual development to be fundamentally incompatible, and consequently seek to improve citizens' cultural level by introducing hierarchical institutions.

Unfortunately, there is an important gap in recent scholarly discourse regarding this particular aspect of liberal democracy. Neither the debate between John Rawls and his communitarian critics nor the ongoing discussion of the globalization of American values adequately addresses the fundamental critique of democratic culture advanced by the aesthetic critics.[6] Rawls and his critics, in focusing primarily on questions of justice, tend to treat culture either as a constitutive element of one's identity or as a spur to civic virtue. They generally do not discuss the relationship between liberal democracy and culture comprehensively—which would require concentrating on more than culture's particular relationship to *justice*. Specifi-

---

5. Joseph Raz, *The Morality of Freedom*, 420, 426.

6. Rawls's argument is contained primarily in *A Theory of Justice* and *Political Liberalism*. For the communitarian critique, see Michael J. Sandel, *Liberalism and the Limits of Justice;* Alasdair MacIntyre, *After Virtue;* and Michael Walzer, *Spheres of Justice.*

cally, the complex relationship between liberal democratic forms and full individual development receives short shrift.

Writers on globalization tend to be more sensitive to the broader implications of culture. Whether the tension between America's values and those of traditionalist societies is cast as "jihad vs. McWorld," "the Lexus and the olive tree," or "the clash of civilizations," scholars in this field are keenly aware of how cultural differences structure world conflict.[7] However, the questions such researchers tend to ask center on, for example, the links between globalization and Americanization, or the appropriateness of promoting liberal democratic values in traditionalist societies. While these are crucial issues, no one has adequately assessed the advantages and disadvantages of modern liberal democracy from the point of view of the aesthetic critics, whose arguments focus not so much on the extension of American democracy, but on the inherent weaknesses of that regime.

I have written this book for readers who, while interested in these existing discussions, are ready for a more comprehensive evaluation of liberal democracy. With the help of three American novelists, James Fenimore Cooper, Mark Twain, and William Dean Howells, I engage the aesthetic critique of democracy head-on. Ultimately, I conclude that the aesthetic critics, while providing an essential criterion for evaluating regimes, miss the manifold ways in which democratic liberty actually promotes individual development, thereby meeting—to some degree—the aesthetic requirement. I contend that the democratic experience of the world is fundamentally fuller and richer than the aristocratic experience, and serves to develop the democrat's faculties to a greater degree than the aristocrat's. More specifically, the democrat's daily struggle for autonomy in the face of material necessity serves as the basis for significant development, especially in the presence of a vibrant public sphere.

Liberals might question why such a defense is necessary, and argue that the aesthetic critics, by advocating an aristocracy or a strong state, mistakenly offer a political solution to a nonpolitical problem. Individual development, they would claim, is a matter of personal choice, not state action.

7. Benjamin R. Barber, *Jihad vs. McWorld;* Thomas Friedman, *The Lexus and the Olive Tree;* and Samuel Huntington, *The Clash of Civilizations and the Remaking of World Order.* For a more skeptical view of the "culture as destiny" argument, see Fareed Zakaria, *The Future of Freedom,* 52–55.

In an important sense they would be right, for liberal democracy is probably preferable to aristocracy and monarchy solely because of its provision of equal rights to all. However, in evaluating democracy based on the type of citizens it produces, the critics are also correct. If democrats invariably turn out to be mediocre, selfish materialists, is it enough to laud democracy's tendency toward peace and private prosperity? The critics say no, and I am inclined to agree. If a regime fails to produce well-developed citizens in a consistent manner, it remains fundamentally incomplete. It may still be superior to other regimes, but it nonetheless requires improvement.

The advantages of revisiting this debate over liberal democracy are clear. Carlyle and the other aesthetic critics provide an interpretation of democracy unclouded by many of the concerns that drive modern criticism. For example, most of the critics do not contest democracy's ability to ensure peace and prosperity, nor do they take issue with democratic justice, which in their opinion is of secondary importance. In addition, they write from a secure vantage point, largely free from the blinders of nationalism. They observe the United States—the extreme case of liberal democracy—from afar, and do not fear the immediate globalization of American values. Their critique appears in a relatively pure form, and we can evaluate it in isolation from other antidemocratic arguments. This is not to say, of course, that the critics have no ulterior motives in attacking liberal democracy,[8] or that they have no fear for its spreading around the globe. However, it is generally the case that they couch their criticisms in broad theoretical terms, compelling liberals to provide a correspondingly thoughtful defense of their regime.

After analyzing the aesthetic critique in Chapter 1, I examine three powerful forces within liberal democracy that drive individual development. Chapter 2 discusses how conditions of equal liberty enable citizens to understand the world for themselves, without mediation, thus creating circumstances favorable to individual development. Chapter 3 focuses on how democracy radically restructures the relationship between people and their environment, compelling them to cultivate certain faculties essential for fuller development. Chapter 4 looks at the role of the liberal democratic

---

8. For an account that emphasizes the post-colonial nature of the Anglo-American cultural debate, see Robert Weisbuch, *Atlantic Double-Cross.*

public sphere in expanding and refining citizens' ideas about the world. Taken together, these chapters will demonstrate that we can indeed offer a defense of democracy on the critics' terms without compromising core liberal principles.

Since this book is about culture, a term that derives from the Latin word for tilling soil, a horticultural analogy might help illustrate the trajectory of my discussion of *hominiculture*. Chapter 2 emphasizes the importance of preparing the "soil" of liberal democracy by clearing it of any "weeds" (the vestigial institutions and habits of old regimes) that could choke out new growth. Chapter 3 describes the process of growth itself, in particular how environmental conditions and inner motivations combine to drive individual development. However, even the best of plants will become scraggly without some pruning; Chapter 4 considers how the democratic interaction of the public sphere tends to trim away our ugliest and narrowest opinions, while encouraging our most promising ideas.

Individual Development

Before continuing, it is necessary to discuss the concept of individual development. As I use the term, at least as a working definition, *individual development* refers to the ever-greater realization of one's potential as a distinct human being. Whereas Aristotle assigned the same telos to entire classes of people, such as free men, women, and natural slaves,[9] my conception of individual development recognizes that although all humans share certain qualities (reason, emotions, and so forth), and thus have roughly similar capacities, each person's potential is ultimately unique. Some people find fulfillment in a profession, while others prefer public service, the arts, or even philosophy. Human capabilities are also highly dynamic. In realizing one aspect of our potential, we not only free ourselves to pursue other aspects of our original potential, but we also create new capabilities to explore. The result is that there are few discernible boundaries to human accomplishment, at least in principle.

Of course, not all the critics and novelists I discuss share this view of human flourishing. These differences will become clear as I proceed. Howev-

9. Aristotle, *The Politics*, esp. bk. 1.

er, it is still useful to explain my conception of individual development, for it plays an important role in my overall argument about the effects of liberal democratic institutions.

By its nature, individual development resists definition, as it encompasses and transcends the particular excellences moral and political philosophers have enumerated. It cannot be confined neatly within a table of virtues. It is not coeval with civic virtue, though becoming a good citizen may be a part of individual development. It goes beyond moral rectitude, though full development implies both ethical and ecological responsibility. Nor is it the same as "high culture," though in realizing their potential some people will produce great works of art and music. What one can say, however, is that individual development generally involves awakening one's reason and higher sensibilities, and understanding what ordering of values is appropriate to oneself.

In this respect, individual development bears a close resemblance to *Bildung*, the German romantic ideal of self-cultivation. In *The Limits of State Action*, Wilhelm von Humboldt asserts, "The true end of Man . . . is the highest and most harmonious development of his powers to a complete and consistent whole." Self-development fuses our rational and passionate natures, resulting in a "many-sided and vigorous character." In a similar vein, Johann Gottfried von Herder argues for an expanded conception of *Humanität*, one that includes not only our capacity for reason, but our "finer senses and impulses, the most delicate and most robust health, the realization of the purpose of the world and the control over it."[10]

Perhaps the most influential account of *Bildung* is found in the writings of Friedrich Schiller.[11] In his *Letters on the Aesthetic Education of Man*, Schiller argues that culture is a matter of doing justice to two basic human forces: the sensuous drive and the formal drive. Whereas the sensuous drive constrains us through the laws of nature, "bind[ing] the ever-soaring

10. Wilhelm von Humboldt, *The Limits of State Action*, 10, 12–13, 18; Johann Gottfried von Herder, *Ideas for a Philosophy of the History of Mankind*, in *J. G. Herder on Social and Political Culture*, 267. Humboldt's ideal served as the basis of John Stuart Mill's conception of individuality. See Mill, *On Liberty*, in *On Liberty and Other Essays*, 2, chap. 3.

11. Cooper was particularly enamored of Schiller. After visiting Schiller's birthplace, he penned the following lines: "The schools, and a prevalent taste and the caprice of fashion can make Goethes in dozens, at any time; but God only creates such men as Schiller." Quoted in Preston A. Barba, "Cooper in Germany," 29–30.

spirit to the world of sense, and summon[ing] abstraction from its most unfettered excursions into the infinite back to the limitations of the present," the formal drive constrains us through the laws of reason, "wrest[ing] . . . our condition from the jurisdiction of time, and endow[ing] it with reality for all men and all times, that is with universality and necessity." A third force, the play drive, reconciles the sensuous and formal drive, by "introducing form into matter, and reality into form." The result is "living form," the basis of "beauty." Our reason and our senses become united in play, the activity that makes us fully human. Schiller's famous example of play is the dance, where whirling couples joyfully meld desire with rational autonomy in an ever-changing but consonant whole. As he puts it,

> How is each one at freedom to follow the will of his bosom,
>   And to find out the sole path, as he pursues his swift course?
> Wouldst thou know how is it? 'Tis Harmony's powerful godhead,
>   Changing the boisterous leap into the sociable dance,
> That, like Nemesis, links to the golden bridle of rhythm
>   Every violent lust, taming each thing that was wild.[12]

The conception of individual development that Humboldt, Herder, and Schiller advance emphasizes well-roundedness and the harmonious cultivation of human capacities. In this respect, it adequately describes the sort of character most people are capable of and can strive for.[13] Yet, like Aristotle's teleology, the ideal of *Bildung* requires some caveats, for it is overly restrictive as originally advanced. First, although well-roundedness may be an appropriate end for most people, there are always some whose highest potential lies not in multifaceted development, but in the intense cultivation of one aspect of humanity. Mozart, for example, was hardly a well-rounded person, yet both he and the world were better off as a result. Second, though we should strive for harmonious development, we must recognize that it is often those with the most tortured souls who see life most clearly. John Bunyan, Johann Wolfgang von Goethe, Herman Mel-

---

12. Friedrich Schiller, *Letters on the Aesthetic Education of Man*, in *Essays*, 118–28; Friedrich Schiller, *Schiller's Poems*, 240 (ll. 21–26).

13. See Daniel Walker Howe, *Making the American Self*, for an account of the prevalence in antebellum America of a similar ideal, that of "hav[ing] all one's faculties properly exercised, developed, and disciplined" (127).

ville, and Vincent van Gogh are just a few examples. Finally, harmonious, well-rounded development is an ideal we can only hope to approximate, given the imperfections of this world and of human nature. Humboldt, Herder, and Schiller realized this, but their idealism often overshadowed their realism. In short, any realistic conception of individual development must take seriously the variety of human potentials and the practical limits upon the realization of those potentials.

One might also worry that since the ideal of *Bildung* was originally espoused by writers living in nondemocratic countries, it might be incompatible with democracy. Fortunately, the practice of *Bildung* is not inextricably linked to hierarchical political and social institutions, and in fact is quite consistent with liberal democratic institutions. As this book attempts to demonstrate, this ideal is within reach of democratic citizens, given proper conditions and the aforementioned caveats.[14]

Individual development could be termed "self-cultivation," since it involves a substantial amount of reflection, self-criticism, and lifestyle revision. However, in the midst of unsuitable conditions (for example, slavery, isolation), self-cultivation becomes futile or artificial. One cannot simply will one's own development, for it requires both freedom and active engagement with one's social and natural environments to be genuine. Therefore, I have avoided the use of the terms *culture* and *self-cultivation*—not because they are inappropriate in this context, but because they speak to only one part of the process of development. As we shall see, with the novelists' assistance, true human flourishing depends upon favorable circumstances as well as willful action on the part of the individual.

This added requirement makes the problem of individual development a concern of political philosophy. If we agree that it is better for people to flourish than to remain in a state of stunted mediocrity, then we should consider whether the state can help create the conditions necessary for such flourishing—and whether it is appropriate for it to do so. In general, the aesthetic critics advocate an expansive role for a state or aristocracy in encouraging full development, believing such institutions provide a key elevating influence upon the individual. In this argument, abolishing formal hierarchy and limiting the sphere of governance remove any hope for a well-

---

14. For a similar attempt to synthesize German romanticism with liberalism, see Nancy Rosenblum, *Another Liberalism*.

developed citizenry, since people tend to choose poorly when left to their own devices. Are the critics correct? To a certain degree, yes. However, they overlook how conditions of equal liberty provide a stronger elevating influence on citizens' character than does either an aristocracy or an overbearing state. A complete justification of liberal democracy must include an explanation of how that regime can facilitate individual development *indirectly.* This project will augment traditional justifications of democracy in such a fashion.

Liberalism Assaulted

Why is liberal democracy vulnerable to the aesthetic critique? Though the answer to this question will be developed further in Chapter 1, a brief (and necessarily simplified) examination of certain tenets of liberalism will help identify the weaknesses critics see in both the theory and practice of modern democracy.

The doctrine of modern liberalism arose from the religious and political turmoil of the seventeenth century, and was originally advanced as a realistic solution to the problem of governing a deeply divided society. In a world where widespread disagreement over the ends of life and the requirements of salvation leads to skepticism about the truth claims of any given individual, structuring society around a particular conception of truth or the good life (as in classical or Christian political thought) is inherently risky. This is Thomas Hobbes's premise in *Leviathan,* where he argues that we can avoid civil war only by relinquishing all civil and religious power to a unitary sovereign, who, by serving as final arbiter, prevents factionalism from endangering his subjects' safety. Since man is by nature selfish and vaingloriously confident of his own wisdom, the central aim of government (if the state is to survive) necessarily becomes the maintenance of security, not the cultivation of virtue or the pursuit of noble communal ends, unless the latter are vital to security. The sovereign's laws protect his subjects from foreign conquest and each other's depredations; they are not primarily intended to inspire civic-mindedness or to prod individual development.[15]

15. Thomas Hobbes, *Leviathan,* esp. 183–84, 272.

Subsequent liberals abandon Hobbes's authoritarianism, but they accept his transformation of the role of government. For them, as for Hobbes, government exists to *preserve,* not to shape or elevate its citizens. For John Locke, the insecurity of property claims in the state of nature prompts individuals to enter civil society, the *"chief end"* of which is the preservation of each citizen's life, liberty, and estate. In similar fashion, Thomas Jefferson writes that governments are instituted not to impose a particular religious creed or to create virtuous citizens, but rather to secure the individual rights to life, liberty, and the pursuit of happiness. The U.S. Constitution declares its purpose to be, in addition to unifying the states and promoting the general welfare, to "establish Justice, insure domestic Tranquility, [and] provide for the common defence." Neither education nor the cultivation of virtue is mentioned, making the federal government a solidly liberal institution on paper—especially once the Bill of Rights is added.[16]

The Hobbesian transformation of government's purpose dramatically expands the sphere of individual liberty. As long as the sovereign's subjects obey his decisions in matters concerning security, they are free to live as they see fit: "In cases where the Soveraign has prescribed no rule, there the Subject hath the liberty to do, or forbeare, according to his own discretion." Importantly, religious beliefs and practices are beyond the sovereign's control, so long as they do not impinge upon the well-being of the community (that is, challenge the sovereign's authority). Thus Hobbes is able to defend the "Independency of the Primitive Christians to follow Paul, or Cephas, or Apollos, every man as he liketh best." Locke's argument for religious toleration follows Hobbes's closely: namely, that "seeing one Man does not violate the Right of another, by his Erroneous Opinions, and undue manner of Worship, nor is his Perdition any prejudice to another Mans Affairs; therefore the care of each Mans Salvation belongs only to himself." Moral suasion must largely replace force as the means by which people's minds are influenced—a sentiment deeply embedded in Jefferson's "Bill for Establishing Religious Freedom": "[A]ll attempts to influence [the mind] by temporal punishments, or burthens, or by civil incapacities, tend

16. John Locke, *Two Treatises of Government,* 2.124; The Declaration of Independence, para. 2; U.S. Constitution, Preamble.

only to beget habits of hypocrisy and meanness, and are a departure from the plan of the holy author of our religion, who being lord both of body and mind, yet chose not to propagate it by coercions on either, as was in his Almighty power to do, *But to extend it by its influence on reason alone.*" These ideals become securely moored to the daily life of a political community in the text of the U.S. Constitution, in particular in the First Amendment. In fact, although other nations have embraced similar principles (France, for instance, in its Declaration of the Rights of Man and Citizen), the idea that government exists for a limited purpose—to secure individual liberty—is reflected to its fullest extent in American institutions.[17]

This alone is sufficient to rouse the ire of the aesthetic critics, but the Constitution exacerbates the situation by joining liberalism to *democracy.* Locke and Hobbes were democrats only in the sense that their social contracts require unanimous consent. After the initial covenant, Hobbes endorsed an absolute sovereign and Locke a limited monarchy. In contrast, Jefferson and the Constitution's framers were committed to *democratic* liberty, which is inseparable from popular sovereignty, equality before the law, and the active participation of citizens in the rule of their community. By injecting a substantial amount of democracy into liberalism, the Constitution further endangers the sort of institutions the critics believe are crucial to citizens' full development. Whereas liberalism distances religion from politics, limits the influence of those who wish to impose their views on society, and controls the effects of factions (all in the name of preserving liberty), democracy challenges hierarchical political structures in the name of equality. Working as a team, liberalism and democracy free citizens from both an overly active government and the stifling effects of political inequality.

This combination of liberalism and democracy, the hallmark of the American system, is far more repugnant to the aesthetic critics than either component is on its own. In theory, liberalism can accommodate much of the social and political inequality that the critics claim raises citizens' cultural level. Similarly, in a nonliberal democracy a set of values may be im-

---

17. Hobbes, *Leviathan,* 271, 711; John Locke, *A Letter concerning Toleration,* 47; Thomas Jefferson, "A Bill for Establishing Religious Freedom," in *The Portable Thomas Jefferson,* 251 (italics in the original).

posed upon the citizenry, as military discipline characterized Sparta and virtue marked Rousseau's ideal republic. However, blending the two components excludes, almost by definition, the only elements of each that would seemingly contribute to individual development.

For the sake of clarity, I have concentrated on the Lockean strand of liberal thought, which, though not always embraced by American intellectuals, has worked its way deep into the American psyche—and as such serves as the chief target for the critics. However, at least two other major justifications of liberalism were prevalent during the nineteenth century, and each adds in its own way to the liberal democratic ethos the critics despise. The first derives from Immanuel Kant's moral and political writings, and the second from John Stuart Mill's version of utilitarianism. Kant and Mill arrive at liberalism from dramatically different starting points; for our purposes, both the fact of convergence and the radically different nature of the supporting philosophies are relevant.

Kant begins with the assumption that man is a rational being, capable of acting according to universal moral imperatives. Moral action requires the individual to adopt the moral law as his own out of duty, not compulsion or inclination. A person who does not freely choose to be governed by the categorical imperative (that is, fear or self-interest motivates his actions) is not acting morally, and is no better than a caged animal. Political and social institutions must not stifle people into unthinking obedience. In addition to legal equality and popular sovereignty, the civil state must recognize the principle of freedom: "No-one can compel me to be happy in accordance with his conception of the welfare of others, for each may seek his happiness in whatever way he sees fit, so long as he does not infringe upon the freedom of others to pursue a similar end which can be reconciled with the freedom of everyone else within a workable general law."[18] Despite its close resemblance to the social-contractarian defense of liberty, Kant's argument contains an important new emphasis. For him, freedom is not simply what remains after rights are preserved, but is an essential precondition for both moral action and political association. Though the social-contract theorists recognize the necessity of freedom for genuine consent, Kant in-

---

18. Immanuel Kant, "On the Common Saying: This May Be True in Theory, but It Does Not Apply in Practice," in *Kant: Political Writings*, 74.

vigorates this element of liberal theory. In fact, his justification of (democratic) liberty could be considered the strong form of the liberal argument, as opposed to the weaker, more negative defense of liberty found in social-contract theory. As such, it proves more resistant to the challenges of those who wish to restrict liberty in the name of culture.

Few of the critics under consideration engage Kant directly, for their eyes tend to be on the United States, which received Kantian notions primarily via the filter of the New England Transcendentalists.[19] However, if their critique is to be taken seriously, it must be strong enough to damage not just Lockean liberalism, but the invigorated post-Kantian liberalism that inextricably links moral action to freedom. If the aesthetic critics can find a weak point in *that* theory of liberal democracy, then they will have accomplished their mission.

One could also defend democratic liberty on utilitarian grounds. Mill, for example, argues that allowing extensive individual liberty and freedom of discussion is, in the long run, of great utility to society, and that any attempt to restrict self-regarding actions, though perhaps useful in the short term, actually decreases overall utility. In practice, this reasoning results in a political system similar to those of Kant and the social contractarians, in which "rights" and an extensive sphere of personal liberty are protected. In fact, utilitarian liberalism found its way into American discourse relatively early in the nation's development, though it never dominated American thought as Lockean liberalism did. For example, the author of the 1837 manifesto of the *United States Magazine and Democratic Review* bolsters his case for liberal democracy with utilitarian reasoning. Rejecting "all self-styled 'wholesome restraints' on the free action of the popular opinion and will," he argues that "the main object with reference to which all social institutions ought to be modelled is undeniably, as stated by the democrat [Jeremy Bentham], 'the greatest good of the greatest number.'" Although utilitarianism is subordinated to rights-based reasoning both in this essay and in American discourse as a whole (especially during the nineteenth century), it is important to remember that the aesthetic critics are evaluating a regime that has several possible justifications—one of which draws heavily upon utilitarian reasoning.[20]

19. See Ralph Waldo Emerson, "The Transcendentalist," in *Selected Essays*, 246.
20. Mill, *On Liberty*, 13–19; "An Introductory Statement of the Democratic Principle," reprinted in Joseph L. Blau, ed., *Social Theories of Jacksonian Democracy*, 22–23.

Conceivably, a utilitarian would modify his calculus if the critics made compelling arguments against the social utility of liberty. One could certainly imagine our utilitarian becoming convinced that cultural development deserves a privileged place in his cost-benefit analysis, and that such development is inconsistent with extensive liberty. James Fitzjames Stephen makes just such a case against Mill in *Liberty, Equality, Fraternity,* arguing that extreme liberty of thought and discussion, rather than leading to truth and the cultivation of individuality, instead produces skepticism, apathy, and conformity. Mill is mistaken, Stephen maintains, in assuming that "persecution in all cases proceeds on a theory involving distinct intellectual error." In addition, he notes that "[f]ew things give men such a keen perception of the importance of their own opinions and the vileness of the opinions of others as the fact that they have inflicted and suffered persecution for them." With regard to individuality, he contends that "there are and always will be in the world an enormous mass of bad and indifferent people," who will contribute nothing valuable except under "compulsion or restraint." If we truly want people to think for themselves and orient their minds toward the truth, the last thing we should do is remove all legal restraints: "It would be as wise to say to the water of a stagnant marsh, 'Why in the world do not you run into the sea? you are perfectly free. . . .'"[21]

Utilitarianism seems more amenable to compromises over liberty than either Kantian or Lockean philosophy is. As a result, the critics may win an easy battle against liberal democracy when engaging utilitarians. However, their arguments will not receive adequate testing unless they face a more robust version of liberalism: social-contract theory infused with a Kantian spirit.

For this reason, it makes sense to square off the critics against Lockean/Kantian liberalism, not the utilitarian variety. However, what matters most is whether liberal institutions can be justified in general—not whether particular Lockean, Millian, or Kantian institutions can be justified. The question at hand is whether a regime based on equal liberty and limited by a wide range of individual rights and liberties will tend to produce well-developed citizens. The critics harp on the detrimental effects of liberal democratic political structures on individual development, and I shall try

21. James Fitzjames Stephen, *Liberty, Equality, Fraternity,* 23, 28–29.

to defend liberalism—especially the more robust version—against their challenges. To rebut the critics' charges, and to demonstrate negative liberty's positive effects on individual development, I will augment existing justifications of liberal democracy with an additional set of arguments—arguments that require a deeper understanding of the complex relationship between liberty and democratic life.

Political Theory and the Novel

Political philosophy, as traditionally understood, concerns itself not only with the design of institutions and the administration of justice, but with the ends of human existence, and how social life makes achieving those ends possible. Thus classical thought treats the polis as crucial to the cultivation of virtue, just as Christianity emphasizes the importance of the church congregation for the individual's spiritual life. Both philosophies contain a significant degree of anthropological thinking—that is, investigation into the empirical relationship between institutions (the polis or church) and human behavior (in this case, the realization of human potential). In contrast, modern liberal democratic thought is less concerned with the actual practice of democracy than with the discovery or construction of formal rights. As long as citizens respect others and abide by the law, they are considered largely free to do as they please.

Social democrats are quick to attack modern liberals for their bias in favor of formal rights, pointing out that formal equality is meaningless without its complement, substantive equality. Unless people have the basic resources (food, clothing, shelter, education) necessary to exercise their formal rights, those rights are next to useless. In calling for an Economic Bill of Rights in his 1944 State of the Union address, President Franklin Delano Roosevelt declared, "We have come to a clear realization of the fact that true individual freedom cannot exist without economic security and independence. 'Necessitous men are not free men.' People who are hungry and out of a job are the stuff of which dictatorships are made."[22] Indeed, the New Deal as a whole reflects FDR's concern that formal rights provide little relief on their own. Unless legislators understand how liberal institu-

22. Franklin Delano Roosevelt, "Address on the State of the Union," January 11, 1944.

tions and citizens interact in daily life, laws will continue to undermine the very principles they proclaim.

Liberal theory has a similar weakness concerning citizens' development as human beings. Content with leaving people to their own devices, as long as they obey the law and do not harm each other, liberal theorists pay little attention to whether their institutions aid or impede individual development in practice. They are unaccustomed to handling such questions, which involve a complexity at odds with the elegant simplicity of most of their formulas (for example, equal rights for all). As such, they are of little assistance in answering the critics' charges.[23]

Democratic *novelists,* however, can be instrumental in rebutting the aesthetic critique. Before explaining why, let me make clear that the primary concern of this book is whether liberal democracy can be justified on aesthetic grounds. Whether narrative fiction can be of assistance in this endeavor is a secondary concern. Consequently, although I would like to discuss at great length a number of issues surrounding the interpretation of political novels, to do so here would prove distracting. What follows, then, is a brief, and by no means comprehensive, justification for using novels to understand politics.

Unlike democratic political theorists, novelists focus on the rich detail of everyday life, and they take a greater concern with how democratic life is actually lived. Unlike social scientists, who also seek to understand ordinary life, novelists do not make generalizations based on a superficial understanding of a large number of cases. Nor are novels merely fictional case studies or biographies. To be sure, both of these media lend themselves well to in-depth investigation, and biography in particular has the advantage of the narrative style, but both biographers and case-study researchers are limited to evaluating their subjects' observable acts and statements. Ultimately, even the most skilled researcher can only speculate as to the true motivations of his subjects. Even the most candid interview will reveal only the

---

23. Wai Chee Dimock has argued in *Residues of Justice* that most philosophical accounts of justice are inattentive to the "residues" their universal principles fail to encompass. Literature, she maintains, can better handle the actual complexity of the world. Though her case is somewhat overstated (political philosophers—especially Aristotle—are usually quite aware of the residues of justice), her central insight (at base an Aristotelian one) is nonetheless sound.

interviewed person's understanding of her own motivation, which at best only approximates the causal mechanisms at work. Such investigative limitations hinder biographers and case-study researchers from drawing general conclusions from their research.

Novelists are subject to fewer restraints. They are uniquely able to draw broad conclusions about the human condition from analyzing a small number of subjects. Of course, these subjects are fictional, but that is precisely why the novel is valuable for understanding life. Because the novelist creates his characters from the ground up, he is not limited to observing their external actions. He knows their motivations because he has constructed every aspect of their being. They are (almost) fully known to him.[24] In addition, since novels are written in narrative form, they preserve more of the intricate meaning and symbolism found in everyday interaction than do philosophical treatises, which are restricted by academic customs of expression. Such customs are helpful in preventing patently false ideas from entering academic discourse, but they also compel scholars to write in an orderly, transparent fashion. Reading good literature reminds us that wisdom is not easily boxed up in prosaic prose. Some ideas are communicated better through evocation and symbolism than through clinical examination—which by its nature is selective and partial, leaving much meaning unseen.

It is here that novels and poetry can be useful complements to scholarly discourse—not by transcribing superficial reality, but by hinting at the deeper meaning of things. In our case, novels are simply better than philosophical treatises at capturing the complexity of democratic life, as well as the forces propelling and hindering individual development. As long as novelists' characters are plausible representations of democratic people, the fact that they are, strictly speaking, fictional poses few difficulties. It may even be the case that fictional interpretations of reality may give us more

24. Literary critics often debate whether it is legitimate for authors to assume this much knowledge of characters, and to base generalized conclusions on what might be only figments of their imagination. While it is true that we can only know ourselves (and the characters we create) incompletely, it does not necessarily follow that injecting authorial commentary regarding the inner thoughts and motivations of characters is poor narrative style. On this point, see Wayne C. Booth, *The Rhetoric of Fiction;* and Irving Howe, *Politics and the Novel,* 20–21.

interesting insights into the human condition than the best of empirical studies.

Maureen Whitebrook writes that political theorists tend to use literary examples either as illustrations for arguments or as tools for moral education. My approach is closer to the former than the latter, as I seek to understand the relationship between liberal democracy and individual development. However, I attempt to avoid "the old practice of trawling literature for political illustrations," since novels have a much richer contribution to make to our understanding of democratic life than an occasional apt quotation. As Whitebrook puts it, "There is a connection between thinking about politics and the 'real world' of politics which is mediated via the imagination. Imagination can be expressed through and exercised by literature. There is, then, an interrelationship and movement—political thought—imagination assisted by literature—political life." One might even say that it is impossible to bridge the gap between political theory and political practice *without* the sort of concrete-imaginative thinking that novels embody. As John Horton and Andrea Baumeister note, narrative is central to many political philosophies, including those of Hobbes and Locke, "whose theories are cast in the form of stories about the transition from a (largely) hypothetical state of nature to political society."[25]

In this context, it is important to recall Alasdair MacIntyre's observation that man is by nature a "story-telling animal," who "becomes through his history . . . a teller of stories that aspire to truth." Unless we can express in stories the truths we sense or logically deduce, our understanding of those truths will remain incomplete. For example, students reading Kant and Rawls for the first time often complain that neither philosopher adequately explains how his elegant theory relates to actual political practice. One wonders whether, if Kant and Rawls were better storytellers, they could demonstrate more effectively how to connect their theories to the workings of the real world.[26] In fact, Susan Mendus does just that, comparing the re-

25. Maureen Whitebrook, "Taking the Narrative Turn: What the Novel Has to Offer Political Theory," in John Horton and Andrea T. Baumeister, eds., *Literature and the Political Imagination,* 32, 44; Horton and Baumeister, "Literature, Philosophy, and Political Theory," in Horton and Baumeister, eds., *Literature and the Political Imagination,* 15. For an account of the civic use of literature, see Martha Nussbaum, *Poetic Justice.*
26. MacIntyre, *After Virtue,* 216. To be fair, from the standpoint of narrative Kant's es-

lationship between literary and philosophical theory to what Rawls calls reflective equilibrium, the state reached "after a person has weighed various
proposed conceptions [of justice] and he has either revised his judgments
to accord with one of them or held fast to his initial convictions." Mendus
speculates: "There may be [a similar] equilibrium which results from the
interplay of the descriptions contained within the narrative and the principles or rules which make that description plausible or acceptable . . . it
would be the role of narrative to provide descriptions, and the role of philosophical theory to expose the conceptions of human nature which are pre-
supposed by those descriptions."[27] At any rate, it is clear that although political theorists are well aware of the complexities of everyday life, their
chosen modes of expression limit them to analyses that are relatively abstract. Augmenting their work with that of novelists produces an understanding of democracy marked by both greater concreteness and—perhaps
more notably—wider significance. Richard Posner, for example, describes
great works of literature as having a "mysterious capacity to speak to people who live in different times, which often means in different cultures,
from the time and culture in which the work was written. These works have
a measure of *universality*—it is what enables them to pass the test of time,
to survive into cultures remote from those of their creation." Martha Nussbaum concurs, arguing that the best novels are as philosophically significant as the best abstract treatises, where philosophy is understood as the
"pursuit of truth." In fact, she contends that "[t]he very qualities that
make . . . novels so unlike dogmatic treatises are, for us, the source of their
philosophical interest." The peculiarity of the novelistic form, combined
with novels' "mysterious, various, and complex content," helps complete
the understanding of the world given to us by traditional philosophy.[28]

It is possible, however, to overstate the case for using novels instead of

---

say "Theory and Practice" is a helpful adjunct to his *Grounding for the Metaphysics of Morals,*
as the essay fleshes out the consequences of his moral theory for the actual workings of liberal society. Similarly, Rawls's *Political Liberalism* exhibits greater narrative sophistication
than his *Theory of Justice.*

27. Rawls, *Theory of Justice,* 43; Susan Mendus, "What of Soul Was Left, I Wonder? The
Narrative Self in Political Philosophy," in Horton and Baumeister, eds., *Literature and the
Political Imagination,* 65–66. Martha Nussbaum advocates a version of reflective equilibri-
um similar to Mendus's in *Love's Knowledge,* chap. 6.

28. Richard Posner, *Law and Literature,* 7; Nussbaum, *Love's Knowledge,* 29.

traditional theoretical modes. In *Real Toads in Imaginary Gardens,* Maureen Whitebrook argues,

> Attention to the novel makes it plain that an extreme individualism is an untenable position, and that the integration of the individual into a social order with a necessary political dimension and, accordingly, political obligations and responsibilities, is an essential element in individual identity. Political theory deals in rather stark generalizations: the individual as subject to political authority or resistant to it. Literature depicts the solitary individual . . . outside of the established order, but requiring some sort of political and social order to realize their identity as individuals.[29]

Although Whitebrook is correct that political theory tends to deal in generalizations, her suggestion that political theorists naively believe these generalizations to be fully true is troubling. It is difficult to name a political theorist who actually defends extreme individualism, or who believes people can realize their individuality in the total absence of "political and social order." It seems more accurate to stress the differing aims and methodologies of fiction and political theory, and how these different pursuits cause novelists and political theorists to emphasize certain aspects of reality over others. The problem of overgeneralization is the result not of ignorance, but of inherent methodological limitations.

Finally, it bears noting that the rise of the novel as a literary form coincided with the rise of modern democracy and the middle class. Its appeal is more popular than abstract treatises, a clue to its value in our case. To appeal broadly, a novel must say something of importance to a vast populace, and is likely to have some universalistic pretensions. Novelists usually do not write merely for fun, but rather to convey insights and experiences with which readers can identify and in which they can share. This has the added value of making novelistic examples helpful as the starting points for common deliberation. Nearly everyone has read *Huckleberry Finn,* for example. However, any claim to universalism in a novel is inherently suspect, since the novel as literary form is a historical artifact with identifiable origins and traceable development. Even broad appeal cannot be equated with univer-

29. Maureen Whitebrook, *Real Toads in Imaginary Gardens,* 133.

sal appeal, since that would require the acceptance of a novel's insights by all generations of mankind, past, present, and future.

The same can be said of liberal democracy. Even if, as Francis Fukuyama has asserted in *The End of History and the Last Man* (following Hegel and Kojève), liberal democracy marks the end of history, it can be considered universal only in the sense of a universal goal, not a universally and immediately applicable principle. Liberal democracy is not for all peoples at all times, and it would be arrogant to assume otherwise. However, it does have a shot at being the best possible regime. The genre of literature most characteristic of the regime—novels—will help us determine that.

Allies in the Aesthetic Defense of Democracy: Cooper, Twain, and Howells

Cooper, Twain, and Howells are hardly the only novelists to investigate the relationship between democratic institutions and individual development, but their writings complement each other effectively and together contain some of the best insights into the promise and practice of American democracy. Because, as Americans, they observed firsthand the nation in which liberal democracy has best flourished, they could draw conclusions that are relevant not only to the American experience, but to liberal democracy in general—at least insofar as America's experience with liberal democracy can be considered typical or illustrative of the general characteristics of the regime. (This is hardly an uncontroversial assumption, but it is far from false.) Furthermore, as nineteenth-century writers, they offer the unique critical perspective of those who have witnessed radical social transformations: since the old ways had not faded from memory, and the new ways were still new (that is, no ideological consensus had hardened), the new ways were not taken for granted. Unlike many modern Americans, who tend to dismiss opposition to democracy as irrational traditionalism, Cooper, Twain, and Howells found nothing unusual in the practice of exposing democracy to critical examination—especially given the number of acerbic European travel narratives published during their century. Most importantly, though, all three took seriously the aesthetic critique of democracy, and in struggling to define the nature of the American experience they provide a compelling response to the critics.

Each novelist contributes different elements to this response. Cooper, for example, is helpful in understanding the opportunities for and obstacles to individual development in situations where liberty and equality, as on the frontier, are in their extreme forms. Twain, meanwhile, provides a powerful analysis of the barriers to individual development in both hierarchical and egalitarian societies, and offers a shrewd analysis of the relationship between modern technological thinking and individual development. For his part, Howells concerns himself with the impact of America's transition to urban capitalism on the individual. Taken together, the three novelists present a relatively comprehensive portrait of democratic conditions and their effect on individual development. As such, they provide a valuable corrective to traditional liberal thought, and serve as solid allies against the aesthetic critics.

One might wonder why I have excluded Nathaniel Hawthorne, Herman Melville, Henry James, and many other worthy American writers from my study. In truth, I have no conclusive answer, and I would be foolish to attempt to provide one. An exhaustive study of democratic liberty would certainly consider these writers, as their work indubitably enhances our understanding of democratic life. However, with reference to the specific question at hand, Hawthorne, Melville, and James are less directly relevant than Cooper, Twain, and Howells. Hawthorne, for example, is more useful in understanding the lingering legacy of Puritanism and the psychological roots of pride, guilt, and anxiety than in discovering the specific links between liberal democratic institutions and individual development. For his part, Melville delves into the nature of evil, innocence, and revenge, and his characterizations of Ahab, Billy Budd, Claggart, and Captain Delano give us great insight into the human condition. However, his writings—like Hawthorne's—operate on a different plane than is necessary for replying to the aesthetic critique. James seems more appropriate to include, given his attention to the interplay of American and European norms. Yet even he does not address the question of liberal democracy's effects as pointedly as Cooper, Twain, and Howells do. The transformations James's innocent Americans undergo as they experience the older, more refined cultures of Europe, though profound, cannot easily be attributed to the effects of liberal democracy. On this point, Howard Mumford Jones observes,

> Unlike Howells, James is no egalitarian; and furthermore, his American travel books have an anthropological air as of a cultivated ex-

plorer reporting on the naïve customs of rude, colonial tribes. It is true that in the confrontation of Europe and America James finds many Americans, however simple, morally superior to corrupt European families like the Bellegardes in *The American*. Against this truth one must set his passionate admiration for the British upper class with their country houses, their infinite leisure, their taste, and their courtesy. . . . [The Jamesian universe] is a world without labor, without industry, without commerce, without religion, and without political responsibility.[30]

In comparison, Howells sets up the tension between innocence and experience within the confines of American democracy (see, for example, the discussion in Chapter 2 on Silas Lapham and Bromfield Corey), thereby isolating the transformative effects of liberalism.

It is more difficult to exclude the Transcendentalists from this study. Ralph Waldo Emerson, Henry David Thoreau, and Walt Whitman all emphasize themes that recur in the work of Cooper, Twain, and Howells, such as the importance of self-reliance, the dignity of autonomous labor, and the ultimate harmony of man and nature. Like these novelists, Emerson, Thoreau, and Whitman all embrace democratic institutions while rebuking democratic man for not living up to his potential. In fact, at times it seems the Emersonians could make a better case against the critics than the novelists can. Whereas Cooper often stumbles through his prose and does injustice to his great themes, Emerson's style is enviable. Whereas Twain hides his message behind folksy humor, Thoreau argues in a direct, deliberate fashion. And whereas Howells tends to be fastidious, Whitman celebrates democratic man in all his crudeness. Why, then, should they not play a part in this project?

First, they are primarily essayists and poets, not novelists, and they concern themselves with what can be expressed through poetry and evocative essays. Though attentive to the complexity of democratic life, they cannot capture it quite as well as the novelists do. Yet this is hardly a knockdown argument, especially given the eloquence with which the Emersonians describe democratic people, such as the Canadian woodchopper who visits Thoreau at Walden Pond.[31] Nor is it especially productive to point out

30. Howard Mumford Jones, *Jeffersonianism and the American Novel*, 38.
31. Henry David Thoreau, *Walden*, 93–98.

Emerson's rather flippant dismissal of the concept of evil, or the potentially dangerous effects of Emersonian individualism on social cohesion, for neither of these critiques would rise high enough to engage the Transcendentalists on their own level. Despite the shortcomings of these arguments, however, the fact that we are still debating Emerson's status as a democratic thinker suggests that there remains something of a tension between Emersonianism and traditional liberal democratic thought.[32]

Transcendentalism's mystical underpinnings make it peculiarly immune to criticism, since the Transcendentalist can always escape amidst finer abstractions. However, though it is beyond the scope of this project to determine the ultimate veracity of the Transcendental vision, it is possible to identify key areas of substantive (not just formal) difference between Emerson and traditional liberal democratic theorists—differences that explain why Emerson and his disciples do not enjoy the lion's share of my attention.

Let me first mention the awkwardness in labeling Thoreau and Whitman "Emersonians," or even "Transcendentalists." Both Thoreau and Whitman recoil from certain aspects of Emersonian thought, while significantly redefining others. However, neither man would be of much interest if his Emersonian core was not intact. Each man's genius arises from and is sustained by a variant of Emersonian Transcendentalism, and it is this common characteristic that I wish to emphasize—with the important caveat, of course, that I am simplifying things.

The first feature that sets the Transcendentalists apart is that for Emerson—and, to a lesser degree, Thoreau and Whitman—the cultivation of individuality involves more than establishing one's autonomy within a sea of conformity. It also requires participation in the Over-Soul, the transcendent essence that binds us to each other and to Nature. This is what distinguishes Emersonian self-culture from other conceptions of individ-

---

32. See Newton Arvin, "The House of Pain," in Milton R. Konvitz and Stephen E. Whicher, eds., *Emerson: A Collection of Critical Essays*, 46–59; and Perry Miller, "Emersonian Genius and the American Democracy," in Konvitz and Whicher, *Emerson*, 72–84, for insightful commentary on these critiques. John Carlos Rowe offers a stinging critique of how Emerson's Transcendentalism is fundamentally incompatible with his advocacy of social reform—a critique that bears some similarity to my own, though with a different focus. Rowe, *At Emerson's Tomb*, chap. 2. George Kateb has spearheaded the recent effort to claim Emerson and the Transcendentalists as democratic theorists once and for all, most notably in *The Inner Ocean* and *Emerson and Self-Reliance*.

ual development. It does not end with the full development of the individual person, as Schiller, Mill, and others argue, but calls for the transcendence of one's own person for the sake of union with Nature—what George Kateb terms "impersonal individuality." If one questions the metaphysical foundations of Emersonianism, however, much of the Transcendentalists' motivation for undermining traditional authority, dispelling cant, and advocating egalitarian institutions is lost. If there is no Over-Soul coursing through each of us, then there is no solid grounding for democracy—a regime that is valuable to the Transcendentalists precisely because it best enables each person to develop according to Nature's design. As Thoreau notes, American institutions are "very good" only when seen "from a lower point of view." From the highest viewpoint, "who shall say what they are, or that they are worth looking at or thinking of at all?"[33]

Yet this criticism is valid only if one denies the metaphysical premises of the Emersonians. For the sake of argument, let us suppose that such premises are valid, that there is indeed an Over-Soul, and that all people are capable of achieving impersonal individuality. Let us take the Transcendentalists at their word, and see whether their justification of democracy is satisfactory. In *Democratic Vistas,* Whitman declares that "the only large and satisfactory justification" of democracy "resides in the future, mainly through the copious production of perfect characters among the people, and through the advent of a sane and pervading religiousness." By liberating people from traditional restraints, democracy makes possible for all "a towering self-hood, not physically perfect only—not satisfied with the mere mind's and learning's stores, but religious, possessing the idea of the infinite . . . realizing . . . that, finally, the personality of moral life is most important with reference to the immortal, the unknown, the spiritual, the only permanently real, which as the ocean waits for and receives the rivers, waits for us each and all." Thoreau makes a similar argument, noting how American institutions make living deliberately—the way of life that recognizes the deep, underlying unity between Nature and mankind—a path

---

33. Henry David Thoreau, "Civil Disobedience," in *Civil Disobedience and Other Essays,* 16. Kateb notes, "The view of [Emerson, Thoreau, and Whitman] is that a democratic society is best justified as a preparation for [impersonal] individuality and is indeed justifiable as the only society in which such individuality can exist as a possibility for all." Kateb, *Inner Ocean,* chap. 3, esp. 96.

open to all. Instead of raising a handful of noblemen above the common masses, he points out, democracy makes possible "noble villages of men." As Emerson notes, the Over-Soul is "present in all persons," and "[p]ersons themselves acquaint us with the impersonal." Though some can perceive the presence of the Over-Soul more easily than others, all possess the required powers of perception—a fact that necessitates a regime that does little to hinder the spiritual life of its citizens.[34]

At first glance, such arguments seem to provide a solid defense for democracy. However, under scrutiny one can detect a significant shift away from traditional defenses of individual rights, limited government, and democracy. Whereas for Locke and Kant, persons deserve respect because of an innate human quality, such as the dignity appropriate to a rational being, the Emersonians define a person's worth in terms of his *potential*—specifically, his potential to rise to the level of impersonal individuality. To the extent that he exhibits the inspiration of the Over-Soul, he is a worthy companion and deserves our attention. To the extent that he disregards the divine element within him, he deserves our scorn.

In this respect, the Transcendentalists are deeply misanthropic. (This is true even of Whitman and Thoreau, who, though more likely to see the transcendent value of ordinary people, nonetheless evaluate them in the same way as Emerson.) The Transcendentalists are misanthropic not because they criticize existing society and point out that we have not actualized our potential as humans, but because they fail to respect man *as he is,* apart from any potential he might have. As Emerson explains, "What we commonly call man, the eating, drinking, planting, counting man, does not, as we know him, represent himself, but misrepresents himself. Him we do not respect, but the soul, whose organ he is, would he let it appear through his action, would make our knees bend." Furthermore, "[m]en cease to interest us when we find their limitations. The only sin is limitation. As soon as you once come up with a man's limitations, it is all over with him. . . . Infinitely alluring and attractive was he to you yesterday, a great hope, a sea to swim in; now, you have found his shores, found it a

---

34. Walt Whitman, *Democratic Vistas*, in *Complete Poetry and Collected Prose*, 959, 970; Thoreau, *Walden*, 72; Emerson, "The Over-Soul," in *Selected Essays*, 212–13; Emerson, *Representative Men*, 5.

pond, and you care not if you never see it again." Since the "privilege and nobility of our nature [resides in] its power to attach itself to what is permanent," it is no surprise that Emerson proclaims "the highest end of government" to be "the culture of men," not the preservation of property.[35]

In fact, Thoreau's frustration with existing man helped drive his great appreciation of nature. In *Walden* he observes, "We are for the most part more lonely when we go abroad among men than when we stay in our chambers," and he contrasts that loneliness with the communion one may enjoy with nature: "In the midst of a gentle rain . . . I was suddenly sensible of such sweet and beneficent society in Nature, in the very pattering of the drops, and in every sound and sight around my house, an infinite and unaccountable friendliness all at once like an atmosphere sustaining me, as made the fancied advantages of human neighborhood insignificant, and I have never thought of them since."[36] One is tempted to pity Emerson and Thoreau, lonely as they were in a sea of humans showing few signs of achieving impersonal individuality. While the Over-Soul seems to burst forth from worms and other lowly elements of nature, mankind proves curiously recalcitrant. Consequently, Transcendentalists find themselves limited to loving humanity in the abstract, and only rarely in its concrete manifestations: the "eating, drinking, planting, counting man."

Of course, some conception of human potential figures into most moral and political theories, but it is usually counterbalanced by a serious appreciation of man as such. Christianity, for example, teaches that God loves all people—even the worst of sinners. They enjoy this love because they are God's creation, not because they have realized their potential as dutiful Christians through faith and good works. Hobbes and Locke premise their arguments on the idea that there is something in every individual—poor or rich, noble or common—worth preserving above all; both prioritize individual preservation (and the protection of one's property) over cultural development. Kant is even more explicit on this point, grounding human dignity in the fact that humans are the only truly rational beings, capable of operating according to a universal moral law. Though it takes a bit of

---

35. Emerson, in *Selected Essays:* "The Over-Soul," 208; "Circles," 229; and "The Transcendentalist," 257. Emerson, "Politics," in *Essays and Lectures,* 561.

36. Thoreau, *Walden,* 86, 88.

contemplation to determine the right course of action in any particular situation, Kant insists that even the most innocent of people will be able to choose correctly. In addition, as humans we can expect others to treat us with respect, even when we seemingly do not "deserve" such treatment. For instance, we must never lie to another human being, even if that person intends to murder our dearest friend. Even the most despicable people are entitled to our respect, without reference to their disregard for their own potential.[37]

Though I have overdrawn this distinction for the sake of clarity, respect for man *as such* shows through only faintly in Emersonian thought. When Emerson, Thoreau, and Whitman extol certain commonplace aspects of democratic life, in reality they are celebrating the transcendental significance of such activity, not the worthiness of democratic life as such. (Again, this is truer of Emerson than of Thoreau or Whitman.) In recognition of the latter, liberal democratic thinkers give priority to individual rights; it is unclear whether the Emersonian argument for rights is independent from the individual's participation in the Over-Soul. The bracing optimism of the Transcendentalists is attractive, much as fire is to a young child, but unless we treat it with due caution, we risk being burned. There is a reason why Nietzsche finds inspiration in Emerson's essays, and it is not because Emerson clings to the liberal democratic tradition. As Nietzsche puts it, "Such a man [as Emerson] instinctively feeds on pure ambrosia and leaves alone the indigestible in things."[38] This compliment reveals not only Nietzsche's affinity for Emerson, but also the fundamental tension between Emerson and liberal democracy. Both men are after something greater, and in their quest they glide over (or in the case of Nietzsche, reject) important foundational elements of liberal democratic thought. Consequently, Emerson and his disciples are of less use in the defense of liberal democracy than are the more solidly liberal Cooper, Twain, and Howells.[39]

There are many nuances to the aesthetic critique of democracy, and perhaps even more numerous subtleties that could be incorporated into a defense. In this book I lay out the general outlines of an aesthetic defense of

37. Kant, *Grounding for the Metaphysics of Morals,* 15, 63–67.

38. Quoted in George J. Stack, *Nietzsche and Emerson.*

39. For a roughly similar criticism of Emerson (and endorsement of Cooper), see David Simpson, *The Politics of American English, 1776–1850.*

democracy. By no means is it a comprehensive defense, inclusive of all authors who bear on the topic. While I discuss at length the implications of equal liberty for class, social status, and a sense of community, I spend less time on how gender, race, and ethnicity affect individual development under liberal democracy. The primary reason for these omissions is that liberal democracy, in theory at least, is race blind and gender neutral. It is, however, not class neutral. Democracy ruthlessly destroys ancient privileges and sociopolitical hierarchies.

My conviction—perhaps it could be called a working assumption—is that a liberal democratic system, *infused with a thoroughly liberal democratic culture,* will affect people's chances for individual development in roughly the same way, regardless of gender, race, or ethnicity. We are, of course, far from this idyllic state of affairs. A quick survey of ethnic literature, for example, reveals countless works about the difficulties of maintaining or recapturing one's traditional identity while living in or immigrating to a world where elements of one's identity become suppressed. Some of this suppression is due to illiberal actions, such as racial or ethnic discrimination. Such actions are not, properly speaking, part of the liberal democratic culture I describe in this book. Ethnic literature becomes relevant to the aesthetic critique of democracy only insofar as it sees race or ethnicity as affecting individual development in a fully liberal democratic polity, devoid of racism and unjustified discrimination. I suspect that under such a regime, one's race or ethnicity would not determine *whether* one fully develops as an individual, but it might affect *how* one develops (that is, which interests one chooses to pursue). These are nuances I shall leave for other, more capable writers to explore.

Ethnic writers have, at times, made critiques of existing American society that strikingly resemble the aesthetic critique I discuss in this book. In his famous essay "The Negro Artist and the Racial Mountain," for example, Langston Hughes laments how aspiring African-American poets discard their own identity in favor of the bland, boring, subway-riding culture of white America. While not a critique of democracy as such, the essay does identify many of the same stultifying features of American life that the aesthetic critics point out. Other authors, such as Martín Espada in "Coca-Cola and Coco Frío," have written about how commercialism in modern America distracts people from what is valuable about their own native cultures.[40] For both Hughes and Espada, as well as for many other ethnic writers, the problems of American culture (consumerism, conformity, discrimination, racism) are detachable from democracy as a regime. In other words, democracy remains a worthy regime choice, though it cannot truly flourish without a vibrant egalitarian culture. Such writers are distinguishable from traditionalist opponents of Americanization, who tend to dislike democracy itself. They are also different from the aesthetic critics I discuss in the next chapter, who see the aforementioned problems as inextricably bound to democracy. They are, generally speaking, allied with the novelists with whose help I defend democracy. However, in focusing on issues of inclusion into democracy, and the difficulties of mediating multiple elements of one's identity, most ethnic writers do not engage the aesthetic critique directly. In fact, an aesthetic critic like Matthew Arnold would argue that even if a liberal democracy like America could resolve its issues of integration and identity (in itself no easy task), it would be no further along the path toward "sweetness and light." This is, of course, not an argument for the irrelevance of the vast resources of modern ethnic literature. It is, however, an argument for prioritizing those authors—in this case, Cooper, Twain, and Howells—who meet the aesthetic critique head-on.

Because of its connections to biological differences, gender is likely to remain salient even in a thoroughly liberal democratic society. However, many of the problems that feminists decry in actual modern life would be less present under a truer liberal democracy. Consistent with the liberal doctrine of rights, rape and other physical abuse would be effectively prohibited. Gender discrimination in job hiring and pay inequities would also be reduced. Even the subtler forms of inequality identified by recent feminist thinkers, such as mental abuse and the uneven division of labor within the two-income household,[41] would be lessened amidst a more genuinely egalitarian culture of respect. As with issues of race and ethnicity, gender would remain relevant to individual development, but less relevant than at present.

Many novelists have written about the relationship between gender and

40. See also how the narrator in Ralph Ellison's *Invisible Man* reacts to "degraded" black culture, represented by Jim Trueblood; to the meretriciousness of Dr. Bledsoe; and to the morally bankrupt white elite.

41. See, for example, Susan M. Okin, *Justice, Gender, and the Family.*

individual development. Harriet Beecher Stowe, for example, emphasizes in *Uncle Tom's Cabin* how the feminine virtues, including those of motherhood, can spur a concern for social justice.[42] Charlotte Perkins Gilman's *Herland*, describing arguably the first feminist utopia, is a thought experiment about the capacities of women when freed from stifling Victorian gender expectations. In addition, Gilman's "The Yellow Wall-Paper," in showing the destructive effects of the rest cure on "hysterical" women, adds indirect support to the argument of Chapter 3 that active engagement, not leisure, is productive of the best individual development. Among contemporary authors, Toni Morrison explores the unique constraints and opportunities for African-American women in an America still fundamentally shaped by the history of slavery and racism. All of these writers—and many, many others working on issues of gender—discuss individual development, and they deserve more attention than I give them here. However, the concern over gender is of somewhat less importance in responding to the aesthetic critique, especially since I am defending a regime that in principle opposes the kind of differential treatment that has inspired much modern literature on gender. As with ethnic literature, the literature of gender is relevant—and would figure prominently if this book were longer—but is not *centrally* relevant.[43]

One can fully trust allies only in retrospect, when they have proven themselves steadfast under fire. Whether I have chosen my allies wisely remains to be seen. We shall confront the aesthetic critics as best we can, by offering a more nuanced, plausible account of the relationship between liberal democracy and individual development. Without further ado, let us see what our opponents have to offer.

42. One striking example is Stowe's treatment of Mrs. Bird in chap. 9 of *Uncle Tom's Cabin.*

43. Charlotte Perkins Gilman, "The Yellow Wall-Paper," in *The Yellow Wall-Paper and Other Writings;* Toni Morrison, *Beloved.*

1

The Aesthetic Critique of Democratic Liberty

"READER, DID YOU EVER hear of 'Constituted Anarchy' . . . the choking, sweltering, deadly and killing rule of No-rule; the consecration of cupidity, and braying folly, and dim stupidity and baseness, in most of the affairs of men?" Thus Thomas Carlyle bewails the "present time," marked by the democratic loosening of all valuable social bonds. For him, democracy, which has swept Europe and is found in its purest form in America, is nothing but "anarchy *plus* a street-constable." As freedom increases, he argues, democrats become narrower in outlook, ignoring higher goods in their relentless pursuit of material comfort. Though America "ploughs and hammers, in a very successful manner," she deserves little recognition: "What great human soul, what great thought, what great noble thing that one could worship, or loyally admire, has yet been produced there?" As for liberty, "The true liberty of a man . . . consist[s] in his finding out, or being forced to find out the right path, and to walk thereon. . . . [I]f liberty be not that, I for one have small care about liberty. You do not allow a palpable madman to leap over precipices; you violate his liberty, you that are wise; and keep him, were it in strait-waistcoats, away from the precipices!" Unless democrats can prove that their brand of liberty can invigorate the soul and encourage individual development, Carlyle is inclined to reject their regime. In his view, democracy leads not only to social and political anarchy, but to an anarchy of the soul that results in petty materialism. What has hitherto been the promise of American life, "[r]oast-goose with apple-sauce for the poorest working man," hardly deserves applause.[1]

With this Carlyle lays the groundwork for an important critique of democracy, one that flourished in Victorian Britain, received inspiration from Plato and Nietzsche, and reached its peak in the early twentieth century. Unfortunately, it tends to be ignored today. In this chapter, I will tease out the main strands of this aesthetic critique, beginning with Carlyle and ending with the high modernists T. S. Eliot, Ezra Pound, and D. H. Lawrence. These writers identify significant weaknesses in familiar defenses of liberal democracy, and we would be wise to consider their objections. In particular, they maintain that liberal democracy, by granting extensive negative liberty[2] to ordinary people, stifles individual development. Give the average person freedom to choose his own life plans, they argue, and he will tend to choose poorly.

The first task is to determine exactly what the critics are criticizing. At times they appear to be targeting democracy as such, while at other times they seem more concerned with the modern synthesis of democracy with liberalism and capitalism—a synthesis found most notably, though not exclusively, in the United States. This latter concern is more relevant, of course, and I shall concentrate on that aspect of the critique. Consequently, my reply to the critics in later chapters will require not just a defense of democracy, but a justification of the whole package: democracy, liberalism, and the free market. This synthesis has interesting implications for religion. Those religions that are "liberal" or "democratic" tend to add support to the basic liberal democratic synthesis, while religions that emphasize hierarchy and deference to established authority remain in tension with liberal equality. While my main focus in this book is not religion—both because the aesthetic critique does not center on religion, and because the question of liberal democracy's worth is distinct from the worth of any particular form of religion—at several points I discuss passages from the novels that highlight the effects of religious beliefs on individual development. Cooper's Jason Newcome and Twain's Huckleberry Finn, for example, are

1. Thomas Carlyle, "The Present Time," in *Latter-Day Pamphlets,* 33, 44, 50; Thomas Carlyle, *Past and Present,* 204–5.
2. Isaiah Berlin defines *negative liberty* as "the area within which a man can act unobstructed by others." Berlin, "Two Concepts of Liberty," in *Four Essays on Liberty,* 122.

prime examples of characters whose belief in illiberal or undemocratic religious creeds prevents them from developing fully as humans.

In this endeavor, Cooper, Twain, and Howells will provide valuable assistance, for although they are cognizant of the problems the critics identify, they have a subtler understanding of how democratic institutions shape character. They are aware of certain tendencies of democracy that the critics overlook—tendencies that promote, rather than hinder, individual development. First, though, let us examine the best case that can be brought against democracy on aesthetic grounds.

One might object at the outset that the critics under discussion are mere cranks or snobs. This may be true. Disdain for America certainly colors Matthew Arnold's writings, and few modern readers would find Carlyle's plan for industrial organization attractive. Yet our distaste for the critics' tone or particular policy recommendations should not distract us from considering their central objections to democracy. My task will be to identify as clearly as possible the critics' common themes, neutralizing in the process many of the particular biases (snobbery, envy, and so on) that initially may have motivated their arguments. From these rather disparate writings, I shall piece together a coherent theoretical challenge to modern accounts of democracy, one whose validity is ultimately independent of the individual critics' personal prejudices. Some abstraction from historical and intellectual context is unavoidable in a project such as this, but fortunately the foundational aspects of the aesthetic critique change little over time. Thus it is possible to treat the critics more or less as a group without doing grave injustice to their particular theoretical positions.[3]

After briefly discussing the Platonic roots of the aesthetic critique, I divide my analysis of the critics into three roughly chronological sections. Each focuses on one radical critic (Carlyle, Nietzsche, Pound) and one or two more-moderate thinkers (for example, Arnold and Lawrence). To be convincing, a defense of liberal democracy must effectively oppose both the harder and softer forms of hierarchy. After all, the moderate (for example,

---

3. Lest the reader think this critique was advanced exclusively by Europeans, it bears noting that Edgar Allan Poe, George Fitzhugh, and the Southern Agrarians, among other Americans, shared some of the aesthetic critics' concerns. Their criticisms, however, were usually not as fully developed or incisively expressed as their European counterparts', and, in the case of Fitzhugh at least, were significantly distorted by racial prejudice.

Mill's clerisy) and extreme (for example, Carlyle's aristocracy) arguments differ more in choice of remedy than in diagnosis of democracy's ills. In fact, those who advance elitist positions under the cloak of "moderate" reform are often more dangerous, since they lull us into accepting a series of small changes that will gradually undermine the existing regime.

The Platonic Legacy

In book 8 of Plato's *Republic,* Socrates famously describes the characteristic features of oligarchy and democracy. Whereas oligarchs value wealth above all, and confine their use of reason to identifying necessary pleasures and "calculating how money may breed more money," democrats emphasize the importance of liberty and free speech. As oligarchy declines into democracy, and people are allowed to do as they like, the distinction between necessary and unnecessary appetites becomes blurred.

Democracy is marked by a "forgiving spirit," and the diversity it allows has a sort of beauty to it, like multicolored cloth. However, this tolerant attitude tends toward anarchy; unequal things are treated equally, and anyone who "calls himself the people's friend" will be honored, regardless of his past record. Democrats are unable to make value distinctions between different ways of life, pursuing unnecessary and harmful pleasures along with necessary ones. Wealth, honor, and wisdom are no longer privileged in such a system. All ends are considered equally worthwhile, and higher goods must compete—often at a disadvantage—with lesser goods in an open marketplace. Democrats abandon moderation and frugality, and call "Insolence . . . good breeding, Anarchy freedom, Waste magnificence, and Impudence a manly spirit." Their excessive love of liberty leads to despotism, as they lift up a champion to overcome all instruments of control, including the very law that secured their freedom.[4]

The critics accept certain of Plato's insights at face value, such as the anarchic tendencies of popular liberty, but they depart from him in an important respect. Whereas Plato thinks democracy naturally descends into despotism, Carlyle and subsequent critics claim that democracy encourages widespread adoption of the oligarchic ideal of wealth gathering. Under con-

4. Plato, *The Republic,* bk. 8, secs. 553D, 557B–558C, 560D–561A.

ditions of freedom, certain ends are more likely to be chosen than others because of their attractiveness to humans as sentient beings. Any person can see the advantages of material comfort, since the desire for such comfort resides deep within the self and is quite demanding (if not sufficiently satisfied, the individual will die). In contrast, it requires greater intellectual effort to recognize the importance of honor or wisdom. As a result, when liberated from outside control, individuals will naturally drift toward the wealth ideal.

By converging on this ideal, people enter a new condition of anarchy, that of the marketplace. Their outlook becomes severely constricted as they concern themselves solely with what advances their own interests. Wealth becomes their only standard of value, and such talents that are not "useful" remain undeveloped. What makes the situation worse is the democratic tendency to ostracize citizens who exhibit exceptional excellence.[5] The result is a comfort-loving, mediocre civilization that has deprived itself of variety.

Although these later critics modify Plato's theory of social revolution by noting the forces pulling democracy back toward the oligarchic standard, they nonetheless are indebted to him for his overall assessment of democracy. They all share his suspicion of liberty, and they advance a number of plans for reining in its undesirable tendencies.

The Victorian Critique

Following Plato, Carlyle argues that democrats, in their passionate love for liberty, come to distrust all social bonds; to rectify perceived injustices within the old order, they "[c]ut every human relation which has anywhere grown uneasy sheer asunder; reduce whatsoever was compulsory to voluntary, whatsoever was permanent among us to the condition of nomadic:— in other words, loosen by assiduous wedges in every joint, the whole fabric of social existence, stone from stone; till at last, all now being loose enough, it can, as we already see in most countries, be overset by [a] sudden outburst

5. See Aristotle, *The Politics*, bk. 3, chap. 13, 1284a17–b35. Benjamin Lippincott correctly notes that Carlyle and other Victorian critics opposed democracy for its tendency toward social anarchy, but he misses the aesthetic import of their arguments. Lippincott, *Victorian Critics of Democracy*, 5.

of revolutionary rage." Carlyle fears revolution, but he truly despises what is left in its wake: the rule of the dim-witted. "It is the everlasting privilege of the foolish," he proclaims, "to be governed by the wise; to be guided in the right path by those who know it better than they. This is the first 'right of man;' compared with which all other rights are as nothing." Resorting to the ballot box may be "excellent for keeping the ship's crew at peace . . . but unserviceable . . . for getting around Cape Horn." Because democratic procedures do not result in the rule of the noble, their value is severely limited.[6]

In Carlyle's opinion, Americans have been saved from utter anarchy solely by their modified English constitution and their "inborn reverence for the Constable's Staff." The fact that Europeans hail America as a model baffles Carlyle. He quotes a fictitious writer, aptly named Smelfungus: "They have doubled their population every twenty years. They have begotten, with a rapidity beyond recorded example, Eighteen Millions of the greatest *bores* ever seen in this world before,—that hitherto is their feat in History!" Before America can take its place among the great nations of history, it must "crack its sinews, and all but break its heart, as the rest of us have had to do." However, that struggle will take place on "other terms than she is yet quite aware of"—conditions that require moderating Americans' excessive love of liberty. Only if the noblest few enjoy political precedence will society survive, for "that is, in all times and in all places, the Almighty Maker's Law." To this end, Carlyle advocates aristocracy and the martial organization of workers under "Captains of Industry."[7]

Carlyle unabashedly rejects democratic liberty, but a number of other Victorian thinkers, including Matthew Arnold and John Stuart Mill, offer more moderate remedies to democracy's ills. For Arnold, the chief obstacle to cultural development is the attitude of "doing as one likes," the spirit infusing modern liberal democracy. Individual liberty is valuable, he argues, but only for the sake of the ends it can help achieve. Left without guidance, people will never reach any appreciable level of culture. (Interestingly, Charles Dickens makes a similar point when he criticizes the Shakers in *American Notes for General Circulation*. For him, liberal democracy simply

6. Carlyle, "The Present Time," 45, 47.
7. Ibid., 43–45.

gives free rein to sectarians, who "strip life of its healthful graces, rob youth of its innocent pleasures, pluck from maturity and age their pleasant ornaments, and make existence but a narrow path towards the grave.")[8]

Arnold compliments Americans for solving both the "social problem," by refusing to admit class distinctions, and the "political problem," by instituting Madisonian checks and balances. Their institutions fit them like a well-tailored suit of clothes, "loose where it ought to be loose, and sitting close where its sitting close is an advantage." However, he writes that political and social problems must not so "absorb us as to make us forget the human problem." In their political and social success, Americans forget there is more to life than peace, prosperity, and liberty: "Do not tell me only, says human nature, of the magnitude of your industry and commerce; of the beneficence of your institutions, your freedom, your equality; of the great and growing number of your churches and schools, libraries and newpapers [sic]; tell me also if your civilization—which is the grand name you give to all this development—tell me if your civilization is *interesting*." The English have aristocrats to remind them of this, but Americans are unhindered in their materialist pursuits. When it comes to the "humanization of man in society, the satisfaction for him, in society, of the true law of human nature," America falls far short.[9]

America's human problem is compounded by the fact that Americans do not recognize it as a problem: "[They] seem, in certain matters, to have agreed, as a people, to deceive themselves, to persuade themselves that they have what they have not, to cover the defects in their civilization by boasting, to fancy that they well and truly solve, not only the political and social problem, but the human problem too." Through "tall talk and inflated sentiment" they convince themselves that they are the best nation on

---

8. Matthew Arnold, *Culture and Anarchy*, in *Selected Prose*, 225–26, 229; Charles Dickens, *American Notes for General Circulation*, 259.

9. Arnold, *Culture and Anarchy*, 251. Arnold quotes Carlyle appreciatively, citing a letter from Thomas to one of the younger Carlyle brothers: "You shall never seriously meditate crossing the great Salt Pool to plant yourself in the Yankee-land. That is a miserable fate for any one, at best; never dream of it. Could you banish yourself from all that is interesting to your mind, forget the history, the glorious institutions, the noble principles of old Scotland—that you might eat a better dinner, perhaps?" Arnold, "Civilization in the United States," in *Civilization in the United States*, 157–61, 170–71.

earth, lacking nothing in their civilization. This arrogance blinds them to their real faults, and consequently hinders individual development.[10]

Because America lacks the elevation and beauty that Arnold sees in truly civilized nations, it is less attractive as a home: "The want [of the interesting] is such as to make any educated man feel that many countries, much less free and prosperous than the United States, are yet more truly civilized; have more which is interesting, have more to say to the soul; are countries, therefore, in which one would rather live." These are strong words, even for Arnold, and they call into question the traditional defense of democracy as a regime that ensures equal liberty. Liberal democracy, on this argument, though providing freedom to both body and soul, does little more. It allows the "common and ignoble, born of the predominance of the common man," to prevail; insofar as it values liberty and equality for their own sake, it cannot meet the basic human need for elevation and beauty. This inability to speak to the soul is a serious mark against democracy when compared to other regimes; freedom and prosperity are not enough to attract those people who rank the needs of the soul above those of the body.[11]

However, Arnold is unwilling to discard democracy altogether. To "prevent the English people from becoming . . . *Americanized*," Arnold turns not to aristocracy, but to the state, which can elevate all classes "by institution and regulation." To him, the modern state is a representation of the nation's collective "best self." Through impartial, rational action, it can establish public institutions to preserve high ideals. Public education plays an essential role in Arnold's scheme, because it is available to all and open to criticism by all. Public schools, because they have a national character, are able to impart ideals and knowledge to children in a way that private schools are unable to match. Because of its national, public character, the state is an appropriate guardian of a society's best principles. Because it is democratically controlled, it does not pose the same threat to the middle class as an aristocratic state would.[12]

However, at base Arnold's theory of education is significantly undemocratic and illiberal. It is undemocratic because it wrests control over the

10. Arnold, "Civilization in the United States," 182–83.

11. Ibid., 181, 191.

12. Matthew Arnold, *The Popular Education of France,* in *Selected Prose,* 111–12, 115, 117–19, 122.

teaching of values and virtues from the hands of local majorities; it is illiberal because it imposes a conception of the good life on children without being sensitive to the varieties of individual experience. Of course, every educational system is constructed around a set of ideals that teachers hope to instill in students (honesty, cleanliness, and so forth), but there is a considerable difference between systems that attempt to limit the imposition of norms, recognizing their contestability, and those that actively and openly attempt to shape students' character. Arnold's views are closer to the latter end of the continuum, being less liberal and less democratic than, say, the ideals of the American educational system.

Like Carlyle and Arnold, John Stuart Mill is reluctant to give popular majorities substantial control over social norms and practices. Though often considered a democratic thinker for his defense of individual liberty, expanded suffrage, and women's rights, Mill is not without his elitist biases.[13] For example, his argument against state regulation of self-regarding acts is motivated primarily by fear of conformity to majority opinion, not a rosy view of the common man's potential. He notes that "the general tendency of things throughout the world is to render mediocrity the ascendant power among mankind." "Public opinion now rules the world," he declares, and "individuals are lost in the crowd." More pointedly, "No government by a democracy or aristocracy, either in its political acts or in the opinions, qualities, and tone of mind which it fosters, ever did or could rise above mediocrity, except in so far as the sovereign Many have let themselves be guided (which in their best times they always have done) by the counsels and influence of a more highly gifted and instructed One or Few." Like Arnold, Mill opposes entrusting government entirely to heroes or men of genius, but he nevertheless believes it should work to create conditions within which exceptional individuals can flourish. After all, "Genius can only breathe freely in an *atmosphere* of freedom." Fighting conformity is so crucial that nonconformity of every kind should be encouraged.[14]

Mill does hope for the general enlightenment of the masses, and his theory of liberty is ultimately directed toward that end. However, until that time comes—and it may not be in the near future—a subtle paternalism

13. For a fuller discussion of Mill's elitism, see Alan S. Kahan, *Aristocratic Liberalism*.
14. Mill, *On Liberty*, 72–74.

is necessary. For example, in *Considerations on Representative Government* he proposes several parliamentary reforms, including proportional representation and plural voting, intended to ensure representation of the educated classes in a body otherwise controlled by the masses. Unless those who labor with their heads are given a disproportionate amount of political power, relative to those who labor with their hands, Britain will go the way of America, where "the first minds in the country [are] as effectively shut out from the national representation, and public functions generally, as if they were under a formal disqualification."[15]

I include Mill among the critics for his pessimism concerning the potential of the common individual to develop fully without outside guidance. For him, liberty is chiefly useful for freeing genius from the majority's clutches; its positive effect on the lives of ordinary people is much less pronounced. Institutions must be arranged, then, to privilege the arguments of the wise, and it is in the best interest of most people (at least in a pre-utopian world) to heed the advice of their intellectual superiors.

What Mill tends to underestimate, though, is how liberty serves not only as a precondition for individual development (geniuses must breathe freely), but as a powerful force impelling even "ordinary" people's development. At times Mill realizes this (like Alexis de Tocqueville, he considers involvement in political life to have an elevating influence on citizens' character),[16] but in general he is skeptical of people's ability to handle liberty well in the absence of a privileged educated class. For this reason, he is in line with Carlyle and Arnold. In the remaining chapters, I will present a more balanced account of the majority's capacity for individual development, based on the idea that liberty has both a liberating and a forming effect.

The Longing for the Heroic

Friedrich Nietzsche and William Butler Yeats add important elements to the aesthetic critique of liberalism and equality. Both are concerned with the increasing mediocrity of the modern soul, which they claim is a result

15. John Stuart Mill, *Considerations on Representative Government,* in *On Liberty and Other Essays,* 328, chaps. 7 and 8.
16. Ibid, 328.

of the masses' being allowed to rule. Both advocate a reawakening of the heroic human spirit and the creation of new values that encourage, rather than stifle, human excellence.

Nietzsche argues that the problem of modernity is linked to the fundamental reformulation of morals that Judaism and Christianity brought about. In earlier times, *good* and *bad* were used to describe the noble and the base; those blessed with noble traits, by calling their own characteristics "good," created a system of values that rewarded human excellence. In contrast, *bad* referred to the low and commonplace—the traits of the mediocre man. Judaism and its heir, Christianity, turned this order on its head. Since both religions were shaped by their adherents' being subjugated to external political authority (that is, Rome), their increasing influence was akin to a "slaves' revolt in morality."

The "ressentiment" felt by Christian slaves toward their masters "turns creative and gives birth to values." Good now becomes identified with many traits formerly considered bad: poverty, weakness, humility. Whereas in the aristocratic morality *bad* was applied as an "afterthought" to everything not good, in Christian morality evil is the starting point. The hatred slaves feel toward their masters causes them to single out the characteristics of masters (strength, nobility) as being more than benignly bad. Such traits are, from the standpoint of the subjugated person, downright evil. Good is then conceived of as evil's opposite, meaning that "[o]nly those who suffer are good, only the poor, the powerless, the lowly are good; the suffering, the deprived, the sick, the ugly, are the only pious people, the only ones saved, salvation is for them alone."[17]

The consequence of this radical shift in morality is that most forms of human excellence are no longer valued—and are in fact despised. For example, if the meek are to inherit the earth, what is the reward for the courageous? Because morality now reflects the "herd instinct," which embraces the commonplace and mediocre, those who have higher hopes for mankind tend to lose their faith:

> For the matter stands like so: the stunting and levelling of European man conceals *our* greatest danger, because the sight of this makes us

17. Friedrich Nietzsche, *On the Genealogy of Morality,* 12–13, 19, 21, 24.

tired. . . . Today we see nothing that wants to expand, we suspect that things will just continue to decline, getting thinner, better-natured, cleverer, more comfortable, more mediocre, more indifferent, more Chinese, more Christian—no doubt about it, man is getting "better" all the time. . . . Right here is where the destiny of Europe lies—in losing our fear of man we have also lost our love for him, our respect for him, our hope in him and even our will to be man. The sight of man now makes us tired—what is nihilism today if it is not *that*? . . . We are tired of *man*.

For Nietzsche, liberty and equality do nothing on their own to further the development of human abilities. Equal treatment does injustice to the unequal, and liberty is worthless without self-mastery. Only the supermen, who are truly each other's peers and who can deal with freedom by creating new values, will thrive in a democratic setting. When common people are entrusted with democratic institutions, they seek the mean in all respects. Though they may feel happy as a result, they never push beyond the mediocre.[18]

Because of this tendency, Nietzsche lists the "rise of democracy" as an important "symptom of life in decline." The problem of mediocrity originated in Judaism and Christianity, and "the *democratic* movement is the heir of the Christian movement." The same herd instinct found in Christianity, with its emphasis on the freedom of the common man, is also present in modern liberal democracy. Though Christianity may initially have triggered Nietzsche's critical spirit, his concern throughout his writings is broader and more secular. As Zarathustra proclaims, "*Everything* has become smaller!"[19]

When presented in 1902 with an anthology of Nietzsche's writings, W. B.

18. Ibid., 13, 27; Nietzsche, *Beyond Good and Evil,* 206, 209. Note also Zarathustra's call for "fellow-creators, those who inscribe new values on new tables," which indicates that Nietzsche's problem is not with equality per se, but with the extension of equality to those unable to overcome existing values. Nietzsche, *Thus Spoke Zarathustra,* 52. For an insightful study of Nietzsche's conception of heroic individualism, see Leslie Paul Thiele, *Friedrich Nietzsche and the Politics of the Soul.*

19. Nietzsche, *Genealogy of Morality,* 121; *Beyond Good and Evil,* 116; *Thus Spoke Zarathustra,* 187. Nietzsche's father and both of his grandfathers were Lutheran ministers, and Nietzsche himself was a model of Christian piety until his late teens. R. J. Hollingdale, introduction to *Thus Spoke Zarathustra,* by Nietzsche, 12.

Yeats wrote to a friend, "I have read him so much that I have made my eyes bad again." As evidenced in his poetry, Yeats shared a number of Nietzsche's concerns, in particular the narrowing and stunting effects of liberty and equality. An Irish nationalist, Yeats sought to lift his countrymen out of mediocrity by reminding them of glorious days past, when peasant, priest, and lord all coexisted in a harmonious and heroic whole. By juxtaposing the commonplace of today and the heroic of yesterday, Yeats both questioned the bourgeois values of modern Irish society, and echoed Nietzsche's discussion of "monumental history," which reminds mankind that "the greatness that once existed was in any event once *possible* and may thus be possible again."[20]

Like Nietzsche, Yeats believed that democratization hinders individual development. For him, when ordinary—as opposed to noble or heroic— people control society's values, mere selfishness and greed replace the desire for true human achievement. In his poem "September 1913," for example, Yeats contrasts the romance of Old Ireland with how the modern Irish pathetically scratch for material comfort. Unlike modern democrats, who in childish selfishness keep track of every paltry cent due them, the heroes of the past were largely indifferent to the material costs of their actions. Faced with drab, meaningless comfort, or a bracing life of heroic, memorable actions, the heroes chose the latter, going "about the world like wind."[21]

When, under conditions of equal liberty, people become narrow and stunted, they are less able—even if wealthy—to break free of stifling communal norms. They cannot think or act for themselves, nor can they create their own values. In his poem "To a Wealthy Man Who Promised a Second Subscription to the Dublin Municipal Gallery if It Were Proved the People Wanted Pictures," Yeats highlights the fear of independence shared even by the powerful. He recalls Duke Ercole of Ferrara, who would sponsor art and music at great personal expense, with hardly a care for what ordinary people might demand. The target of Yeats's poem, the wealthy patron, clearly will only give money if the result will be either profitable or popular. Like the shopkeeper fumbling after pennies in "September 1913,"

20. Yeats, quoted in Otto Bohlmann, *Yeats and Nietzsche,* vi; Friedrich Nietzsche, "On the Uses and Disadvantages of History for Life," in *Untimely Meditations,* 69.

21. William Butler Yeats, "September 1913," in *The Collected Poems of W. B. Yeats,* 106–7 (ll. 1–16).

the wealthy man is unwilling to give without carefully calculating the costs and benefits to himself. Although he is the freest person in the community, thanks to his social status and vast resources, he nevertheless panders to common merchants and gossipy housewives. Being a patron of the arts used to be something to be proud of, and giving was considered part of a noble process of creation. Now, as the multitude presses forth its notions of what is best, the truly good loses its appeal (unless the good happens also to be profitable). Even the elites within this new social structure become vulgar like the masses, or at least too timid to buck the tide of popular sentiment.[22]

Yeats's solution is strongly Nietzschean. As a poet, he exhorts his countrymen to see beyond the values of the bourgeoisie, and to live life more boldly. One must shun the commonplace, he demands, and affirm only those values consistent with human excellence. The ignoble masses threaten all grand endeavors, which rely for their success on the noble man ruling and the common man obeying. Only when the ends of the ignoble are subordinated to those of the noble will society flourish.

Strikingly, though, Yeats does not despise common people *as such*. In "Under Ben Bulben," for example, he recalls with fondness both the nobles and the commoners of yore. Medieval peasants, though lowly, were at least "well made." Unlike the stunted citizens of modern democracy, they knew their proper place in the social hierarchy. They took cues from their superiors, and did not pretend that they were entitled to things, like equality, that they did not deserve. Modern citizens, Yeats implies, though materially better off than the ordinary folk of past centuries, are unfortunately "all out of shape," having no sense for their own proper limits.[23] Like a viola section that plays too loudly, drowning out the rest of the orchestra, modern democrats have lost all sense for the fine, organic harmony of a successful society.

Like the early Victorians, Nietzsche and Yeats decry the mediocrity of democratic life. However, they do not use the state to preserve high ideals, as Arnold and (to a lesser extent) Mill do. For them, the state is simply the formal instrument of mediocrity—where, as Nietzsche's Zarathustra claims, "everyone, good and bad, loses himself . . . where universal slow sui-

---

22. Yeats, "To a Wealthy Man," in ibid., 105–6 (ll. 1–13, 26).
23. Yeats, "Under Ben Bulben," in ibid., 343 (sec. 5).

cide is called—life." The state is created for the "superfluous," those people who do not aspire to the heights of human achievement. It provides for their every need, and ensures that they are satisfied with a comfortable mediocrity.[24]

Nor do Nietzsche and Yeats completely embrace Carlyle—though they share his radical spirit. To them, Carlyle's industrial organization and established aristocracy, if allowed to grow stagnant, would be just as likely to inhibit individual development as Arnold's state. People can indeed be lifted out of their mediocrity, but not by institutions that fail to encourage human excellence in all respects. By praising the well-made in song and verse, poets and teachers who communicate like poets, such as Zarathustra, have a better chance of touching the soul of man.

Despite their differences, Nietzsche and Yeats are better considered allies than opponents of Carlyle, Arnold, and Mill. Though disagreeing on the solution, all five agree that the greatest challenge facing modern democracy is not material poverty or civil strife, but the utter impoverishment of the democratic soul.

Literary Modernism and the Aesthetic Critique

Ezra Pound, T. S. Eliot, and D. H. Lawrence carried the aesthetic critique of democracy confidently into the twentieth century, through world war and economic boom and bust. Like earlier critics, they directed their readers' attention to the increasingly constricted nature of democratic individuality. For them, modernity is devoid of key elements of civilization. It is a "waste land," to use Eliot's term. By eliminating sociopolitical hierarchy, democracy removes all influences that elevate society, leaving people to pursue wealth and comfort without end. In such a context, where money is sought for its own sake, economic well-being serves not to make individual development more likely, but to distract people from that end.

For his part, Pound considered Benito Mussolini the savior not only of Italy, but of all Europe. To him, Mussolini was Italy's Jefferson: destroyer of antiquated values and preserver of the popular welfare. Though the two men's policies differ on the surface, both had the same interest at heart: the

24. Nietzsche, *Thus Spoke Zarathustra*, 76–77.

conservation of an organic society. Had Mussolini lived during Jefferson's time, Pound argued, he would have advocated a strikingly Jeffersonian project; were Jefferson to visit Italy in Pound's time, he would have seconded Mussolini's notions.[25]

For Pound, good government "operates according to the best that is known and thought," while the best government "translates the best thought most speedily into action." Both Mussolini and Jefferson held this view, he argues, despite the traditional association of Jefferson with the idea of limited government. Jefferson, Pound argues, was never fooled into believing liberal institutions are sufficient for good government or gaining knowledge; without a de facto hierarchy that privileges the noble, society will sink to a commonplace level. On this argument Mussolini, by casting himself as a leader capable of enacting policies that conform to the truth, simply made explicit the subtler aspects of Jefferson's thought.[26]

Although Pound was indeed concerned with the efficiency and justness of governments, the element of his antidemocratic thought that is most relevant to this project is his discussion of individual development. For him, a civilized person is someone "who can give a serious answer to a serious question and whose circle of mental reference is not limited to mere acquisition of profit." During America's early years, it was common to find citizens who stood for "a life not split into bits." John Adams, Thomas Jefferson, and others recognized that human development requires the guiding influence of an ideal-preserving elite. However, as time passed, so did the original American elite. Liberal institutions, stripped of the organic hierarchy that had sustained them, could do nothing to prevent the intellectual anarchy of the new age. Ideals became as democratized as the suffrage. Because "[t]here is no more equality between men than between animals," letting the ordinary rule—whether in politics or in intellectual life—is unwise at best. Without the restraining, elevating force of a social elite, liberty inevitably ends in the vulgarization of ideals.[27]

Early America possessed civilization not because of what it claimed to be

25. Ezra Pound, *Jefferson and/or Mussolini,* 34–35.

26. Ibid., 91, 94–95.

27. Ezra Pound, "The Jefferson-Adams Letters as a Shrine and a Monument," in *Selected Prose: 1909–1965,* 118, 122; Ezra Pound, "National Culture: A Manifesto 1938," in *Selected Prose,* 135.

(a liberal democracy), but because of its vibrant social hierarchy, which provided a positive force for enlightenment within a system of negative liberties. Pound challenges us to reconsider the role of liberalism within our society, and to recognize the importance of hierarchy in animating "free" people with noble ideals.[28]

Despite his own leanings away from liberal democracy, Eliot steers clear of fascism. However, like Pound he ruthlessly critiques the "death in living" that characterizes modern existence. Twentieth-century society is shriveled and devoid of life. While people are physically alive, and may even exhibit a certain kind of happiness, their lives lack larger meaning. In *The Waste Land,* Eliot describes commuters crossing London Bridge as so many half-living corpses, breathing and moving but unable to break out of winter's foggy dormancy into a fuller life. Each person looks down at the ground in front of him, oblivious to his surroundings and the possibilities of his life. He, like everyone around him, cares little for anything other than making it to the end of the street—where presumably he will put in his hours and trudge back across the bridge. Not only are the walkers stunted and malformed, but they exhibit no individual qualities. Each is indistinguishable from the rest. All pulse forward together, exhibiting a subtle unity of purpose. Yet this purpose is nothing more than the daily pursuit of petty comforts; no rival values threaten the crowd's unity. Eliot makes this point even more explicit when the poem's protagonist addresses a member of the crowd as "mon semblable,—mon frère!"[29] We are the crowd—all of us.

The bridge scene parallels the opening lines of the poem, which recall winter's soporific ease. During that season, seeds and roots are safely tucked under earth and snow, unmindful of their potential for growth. Until the rains come, the seeds live in this deathlike state. When spring does arrive, and water jolts them awake, life begins anew—but at a cost. To sprout forth as full, healthy plants, the seeds must first give up their happy secu-

28. For a strikingly similar argument, see Walter J. Shepard, "Democracy in Transition," the presidential address for the 1935 annual meeting of the American Political Science Association.

29. T. S. Eliot, *The Waste Land,* in *The Complete Poems and Plays: 1909–1950,* 39 (ll. 60–68, 76). See Genevieve W. Foster, "The Archetypal Imagery of T. S. Eliot," in Lois A. Cuddy and David H. Hirsch, eds., *Critical Essays on T. S. Eliot's "The Waste Land,"* 117, for a similar interpretation of "mon semblable,—mon frère!"

rity under the earth. They must die as seeds in order to become something greater.[30]

Eliot suggests that humans must also undergo a sort of death in order to become fully alive. If people are left to their own devices, however, they will prefer to remain in their stunted dormancy indefinitely. Liberal democracy, which sets citizens free from the beneficial influences of social hierarchy, possesses no resources for prodding people into a greater existence. It gives no institutional preference to higher ideals, allowing common ideas and sentiments to dominate public discourse. In such an environment, the desires that come first to people's minds take precedence, and overwhelm higher instincts. Liberal democrats can indeed feel content, like dormant seeds, but that contentment leads to suffocating complaisance. Like seeds, Eliot implies, humans can be revived if given enough "water." But this life force is unlikely to appear without the elevating influence of hierarchical, organic social relationships. Unless certain nobler ideals come to be privileged in the institutions of society, the commonplace will continue to rule, and humans will continue to trudge their lives away in a wintry fog.

Eliot discusses his social philosophy more explicitly in *The Idea of a Christian Society.* To him, liberalism is a purgatory between the hell of paganism and the (imperfect) heaven of a Christian society. Liberals profess that the state should remain neutral with respect to the competing ideals of paganism and Christianity, sanctioning neither, but in fact liberalism prepares citizens for pagan totalitarianism:

> By destroying traditional social habits of the people, by dissolving their natural collective consciousness into individual constituents, by licensing the opinions of the most foolish, by substituting instruction for education, by encouraging cleverness rather than wisdom, the upstart rather than the qualified, by fostering a notion of *getting on* to which the alternative is a hopeless apathy, Liberalism can prepare the way for that which is its own negation: the artificial, mechanised or brutalised control which is a desperate remedy for its chaos.

---

30. Eliot, *The Waste Land,* 37 (ll. 1–7). On the relationship between death and rebirth in *The Waste Land,* see Cleanth Brooks, "*The Waste Land:* Critique of the Myth," in Cuddy and Hirsch, *Critical Essays,* 88–89.

The only real alternative is a Christian society, which links politics to wisdom and recognizes a positive, elevating purpose for humanity. As Eliot asserts, "[I]t is only by returning to the eternal source of truth that we can hope for any social organization which will not, to its ultimate destruction, ignore some essential aspect of reality." In addition to placing limits on liberal neutrality, such a society must curtail democracy. There should be "rigid agreement as to what everyone should know to some degree and a positive distinction—however undemocratic it may sound—between the educated and the uneducated," and the governing elite must receive a Christian education. The soul is too important to be ignored by political philosophers, Eliot argues, and a laissez-faire attitude toward the soul simply paves the way for totalitarianism.[31]

Like Pound, D. H. Lawrence saw in the work of early American writers (including Cooper) a concern for the human soul unmatched by later thinkers. For him, the "old-fashioned American classics," often considered "children's books," contain a much richer view of liberty than does traditional liberal theory. Throughout American history, he argues, liberty has been conceived of as "breaking away from *all* dominion," a half-truth that has prevented people from discovering and fulfilling "IT," the "deepest *whole* self of man, the self in its wholeness." The major figures of nineteenth-century literature, unlike many of their contemporaries, saw the vital necessity of fulfilling this goal. For both them and Lawrence, pursuit of negative liberty had been useful in destroying the "old master of Europe, the European spirit," but afterward was insufficient for the purpose of individual development. It was clear that America must struggle anew to become more than a "vast republic of escaped slaves."[32]

To be sure, America has never been a fertile ground for anarchy, and Lawrence points out several examples of order imposed on the wilderness of the New World, including Puritan restrictions on religious freedom and Benjamin Franklin's utilitarian prudence. However, none of these forms of restraint has done much for the human soul. Lawrence particularly takes issue with Franklin's overly mechanistic view of human perfectibility. Franklin believed that moral perfection involves cultivating virtues such as

---

31. T. S. Eliot, *The Idea of a Christian Society*, 13, 16, 26, 41, 64.
32. D. H. Lawrence, *Studies in Classic American Literature*, 7, 11, 13–14.

frugality, industry, cleanliness, and humility—and one's progress in each may be precisely measured and recorded. Nor is religion to be neglected, as God exists and will reward good and punish evil. Lawrence argues that Franklin viewed God simply as "the supreme servant of men who want to get on, to *produce*." He notes that Andrew Carnegie could not have designed a more helpful deity. God as provider, the "everlasting Wanamaker": that is the essence of Franklin's religion.[33]

Franklin's obsession with production blinded him to more important aspects of humanity. In Lawrence's words, he "fenced a little tract that he called the soul of man, and proceeded to get it into cultivation." But the human soul is more than the "neat back garden" Franklin intended; it cannot be located in a person's "heart or his stomach or his head." What he tries to fence in with his catalog of practical virtues is actually a small, insignificant portion of the "*wholeness* of a man." He ignores the rest of the soul—the "dark vast forest, with wild life in it."[34]

The "dry, moral, utilitarian" version of democracy that Franklin and others have espoused has done much to undermine European tradition, Lawrence notes, but it fails to inspire any greater, nobler ideal. Despite the amazing material production of Franklin and his fellow citizens, "[t]he American spiritually stayed at home in Europe. The spiritual home of America was, and still is, Europe. This is the galling bondage, in spite of several billions of heaped-up gold. Your heaps of gold are only so many muck-heaps, America, and will remain so till you become a reality to yourselves." Unless we "move in the gesture of creation, from our deepest self," we will remain like "millions of squirrels running in millions of cages." Only by breaking out of Franklin's enclosures and recognizing the deep complexity of our souls can we rise to a higher level; the early American novelists can assist in this process by demonstrating the narrowness of Franklin's ideal.[35]

Although Lawrence did not favor social hierarchy to the extent that Pound and Eliot did, he did recognize the necessity of augmenting liberal forms with an informal elevating force (literature, properly conceived). Like

33. Ibid., 15–16.
34. Ibid., 16–17.
35. Ibid., 26–27.

Pound and Eliot, Lawrence viewed liberty as only the first step toward individual development; without some additional force to pull people out of their narrow mediocrity, society will continue to look much like Benjamin Franklin: "[m]iddle-sized, sturdy, snuff-colored."[36]

The nineteenth- and twentieth-century aesthetic critics of liberal democracy challenge us to recognize both the importance of individual development and the apparent insufficiency of liberal institutions for achieving that end. Elaborating an argument with roots in Plato's *Republic,* they maintain that democratic institutions, though laudable for the tolerant spirit they cultivate, provide few resources for improving citizens' cultural level. Madisonian checks and balances may provide security from the dangers of faction, and may even produce good citizens, like Benjamin Franklin, but they do little to develop the truly human capacities. Only when its institutions are bolstered by a positive, uplifting force can democracy produce well-developed individuals, capable of subordinating material comfort to the deeper needs of the soul.

Though they disagree somewhat over how to augment liberty, the critics are united in their search for a force that can elevate citizens' cultural level. Carlyle's aristocracy, Arnold's state, Mill's clerisy, Nietzsche's superman, Yeats's hero, Eliot's Christian elite, Pound's Mussolini, and Lawrence's novelists—like Plato's philosopher king—are all solutions to the same essential problem. To the critics, whether a nation is prosperous, law-abiding, and civic-minded is only part of the story. A regime must also speak to the soul of man, and produce citizens who are well developed as *humans.* Liberal democracy promises freedom, but it too often devolves into majority tyranny, civility, sectarianism, and/or uniformity. As a result, the critics are willing to discard it or temper it with hierarchical institutions.

Even Tocqueville seems to offer little assistance in this exigency, for he concedes that democratic citizens are mediocre as individuals, and interesting only when considered as part of a nation or as representatives of abstract humanity. "[P]oets in democracy," he explains, "can never take a particular man as the subject of their poetry, for something of medium size, seen clearly from every angle, never has the making of the ideal." Further-

36. Ibid., 19.

more, although the average democrat occasionally thinks broadly, he rarely concerns himself with knowledge not directly connected to practical applications. Consequently, democratic literature tends to be hastily thrown together with little attention to formalities, and its value scarcely exceeds that of newspapers.[37]

Despite their insights into the dark side of democratic liberty, the critics err in supposing that significant individual development cannot occur within liberalism. As I demonstrate in the following chapters, the critics take an overly pessimistic view of democratic liberty, ignoring how liberation creates conditions favorable to individual development. Far from being fundamentally opposed, human excellence and liberal democracy can flourish together.

37. Alexis de Tocqueville, *Democracy in America,* 470–74, 482–87.

2

Democratic Liberation

IN THIS CHAPTER I ANALYZE the first of three features of liberal democracy that promote individual development. I argue that liberal democracy, by allowing people to explore their individuality and engage the world in an unmediated fashion, encourages development in ways the aesthetic critics fail to appreciate. In other words, the very fact of being substantially free from outside control is a crucial precondition for individual development. By this I mean that important decisions must originate from the individual's will, not the dictate of an outside authority; or at least that the individual's will must be actively involved in consenting to or dissenting from a proposed course of action. This *liberating* aspect of democratic liberty, combined with the *formative* aspect of democratic liberty (which will be discussed in the next chapter), can serve as the foundation for genuine individual development.

Of course, a number of theorists and essayists, including Mill and Emerson, have emphasized the importance of freedom for the cultivation of individual talents and capacities.[1] As novelists, however, Cooper, Twain, and Howells offer a richer account of the effects of liberty on ordinary people, and they question the notion that liberty disposes such people toward conformity. Unlike Mill and arguably Emerson, the novelists do not primari-

---

1. See, for example, Mill, *On Liberty,* esp. chaps. 2 and 3; Emerson, "Self-Reliance," in *Selected Essays;* Humboldt, *State Action,* 10; Immanuel Kant, "What Is Enlightenment," in *Kant: Selections,* ed. Lewis White Beck; and Friedrich Hayek, *The Constitution of Liberty,* esp. chap. 2.

ly orient their thoughts around a concern for the achievements of exceptional individuals. Whatever elitism may be found in their philosophies is tempered by a real concern for the development of common men and women. Howells and Twain are, clearly, more reliable on this score than Cooper, whose fussy prejudices in *The American Democrat* place him nearer to the aesthetic critics' camp. However, even Cooper transcends his Johnsonian grumpiness (H. L. Mencken's apt description)[2] in his best novels, which contain vibrant and sympathetic portrayals of democratic life.

This chapter has three central themes. The first involves the novelists' initial reply to the critics: namely, that the latter mistake the effects of one phenomenon for those of another. Many of the undesirable traits observable in democratic citizens, they argue, are a result not of democratic liberty, but of other factors, such as the vestigial habits of older regimes. Unless we have a clear understanding of what causes these undesirable effects, a satisfactory rebuttal of the critics will be impossible. Twain and Cooper are particularly helpful on this point, as much of their work deals with outmoded but residual ways of thinking subtly constraining individual initiative.

The second theme concerns the nature of man when liberated from hierarchy and the conformist pressures of crude egalitarianism. In this context Cooper's Natty Bumppo, who exists on the edge of human experience, illuminates the consequences of increased liberation and the promise of democratic liberty.

The third theme considers the obstacles to achieving democratic liberation. Twain and Howells provide two distinct accounts of the process of liberation, Twain in his portrayal of Huck Finn's encounter with his prejudiced "conscience," and Howells in his discussion of Silas Lapham's revaluation of bourgeois norms. Whereas Twain provides a compelling description of the challenges involved in thinking beyond the confines of communal norms, Howells takes up the specific question of how bourgeois capitalist norms constrain people in modern democracy. In the modern industrial age, where money has become the standard of all value, everything has its price, according to the dominant bourgeois ideology. And we, like

2. H. L. Mencken, introduction to *The American Democrat*, by James Fenimore Cooper, xix.

Silas Lapham, tend to structure our actions accordingly. Yet Silas comes to see beyond this narrowly materialist viewpoint, and his odyssey is still illustrative today.

A Nation of Worms: Feudal Hierarchy in Twain's Camelot

Mark Twain's writings are an excellent source for understanding how modes of thought endure beyond the demise of their corresponding institutions. Even when the tangible features of an oppressive regime have disappeared, its spirit often lingers. By examining situations in which people remain stunted in the midst of apparent freedom, we can better understand the nature and benefits of fuller liberation. In the end, as Twain demonstrates, it matters little whether a hierarchy or a democratic majority is doing the stifling, for the consequences for individual development are remarkably similar.

On the surface, *A Connecticut Yankee in King Arthur's Court* is a delightful satire on medieval hierarchy, and a broad spectrum of readers have relished the notion of modern factory boss Hank Morgan's returning to Arthur's Britain and vanquishing his fabled knights in the name of democracy and progress.[3] While the book's lasting appeal is remarkable, the work is worth little scholarly attention insofar as Twain is merely jabbing at a long-dead set of social practices. On the other hand, though, to consider *Connecticut Yankee* as just another humorous fantasy is to miss its deeper meaning, which we can discover by investigating why Hank's republican dream turned into a bloody nightmare.

The easy answer to the question of Hank's failure is that sixth-century Britain was too primitive to sustain democratic institutions, and Hank implies as much when he devises his plans for a republic. However, it is far from clear that Twain endorses this reason for Hank's failure. Up until the Church's interdiction, for example, everything seems to be moving steadily toward the republican revolution, and at no point—even at the end of the book—does it seem *impossible* to abolish Camelot's feudal hierarchy.

---

3. Carl Van Doren calls the book an "anti-romance," indicating "a reaction from the sentimentalism about the Middle Ages which had recently been feeding on Tennyson's *Idylls of the King,* William Morris's *Earthly Paradise,* the PreRaphaelites, and Pater." Van Doren, *The American Novel,* 176.

The cause of Hank's failure is not that sixth-century people are incapable of self-governance, but rather that Hank underestimates the power of fear, religion, and emotion in subjecting people to authority.

Hank nearly succeeds because he has a keen appreciation of Camelot's problems. He discovers early in the book that England is full of people who, though physically and legally free, slavishly defer to the existing order, without any appreciation of their own individual potential. The doctrine of divine right of kings, Hank finds, had "converted a nation of men to a nation of worms," by making people satisfied with their places in the feudal hierarchy. The system not only treats people like worms, but it makes them believe they are worms, which in effect makes them no different than worms (*CY* 39). Switching metaphors, Hank observes: "[T]hese innumerable clams had permitted [themselves to be dominated] so long that they had come at last to accept it as a truth; and not only that, but to believe it right and as it should be. The priests had told their fathers and themselves that this ironical state of things was ordained of God; and so, not reflecting upon how unlike God it would be to amuse himself with sarcasms, and especially such poor transparent ones as this, they had dropped the matter there and become respectfully quiet" (*CY* 62). Because of indoctrination and habit, not only had these people failed to press for fair treatment, but they could not even conceive of an alternate form of social organization.

Hank's diagnosis of England's ills is confirmed by a visit to Morgan le Fay's dungeon. There he finds a man jailed for protecting his wife from his feudal lord; after years of imprisonment, his fetters had rusted away. Brought face to face with his wife—once the source of his inspiration—the man shows no spark of life, just "weak animal curiosity." Hank notes that "chains cease to be needed after the spirit has gone out of a prisoner." Another peasant, the most recent addition to the dungeon, had been jailed for remarking that "men were about all alike, and one man as good as another, barring clothes." Le Fay had succeeded in suppressing in these prisoners two of the most basic human impulses: love and self-respect. In the name of maintaining the power relationships of her hierarchical society, she had turned thinking, feeling persons into clods of earth. Physical freedom would be meaningless to these prisoners, for their spirit had been trained out of them (*CY* 94–95).

Hank correctly realizes that a republic based on such "freemen" could not long endure. When released from hierarchical control, such people would fare poorly, being for the first time fully responsible for their actions. Since they would have no internal principle of right and wrong to guide them, other than one imposed by the old regime, they would either remain subservient de facto (like le Fay's unchained prisoner) or wander through life aimlessly. Either way, mere physical freedom would be insufficient preparation for democratic self-rule. (It is important to note, however, that Hank's—and Twain's—judgment of English "freemen" does not apply to those who yearn for liberty and attempt to throw off their shackles. These would be true freemen, prime material for democratic society.)

Throughout the book Hank draws comparisons between Camelot and the American South. He notes how, in both societies, slavery degrades the slave, corrupts the master, and makes the ordinary "freeman" subservient to his social superiors. For instance, he watches in horror as peasants track down and hang other peasants, all in the name of serving their feudal lord:

> It reminded me of a time thirteen centuries away, when the "poor whites" of our South who were always despised and frequently insulted, by the slave-lords around them, and who owed their base condition simply to the presence of slavery in their midst, were yet pusillanimously ready to side with slave-lords in all political moves for the upholding and perpetuating of slavery, and did also finally shoulder their muskets and pour out their lives in an effort to prevent the destruction of that very institution which degraded them. (*CY* 181)

Hierarchy in America, like hierarchy in medieval Britain, debases even those who are not at the very bottom of the social ladder. Twain's point is that black slaves were not the only people turned into instruments of the social elite; free whites, who had been indoctrinated into supporting the hierarchy, were degraded as well. In fact, Twain implies that their condition was, in a sense, even worse, since chains were not needed to keep them in line. A republic ostensibly founded on such "freemen" could not (and did not) stand. This puts a new spin on Kant's statement that the problem of organizing a republic could be solved even for a race of devils, so long as they were intelligent.[4] In Twain's view, a republic could be established more

---

4. Immanuel Kant, "Perpetual Peace: A Philosophical Sketch," in *Kant: Selections,* 443.

easily for a race of devils than for Arthurian "freemen," so long as they had a sense of self-worth. Institutions can keep self-interested people in line, but can do little to prompt action by spiritless citizens.

Convinced that "a man *is* a man, at bottom," and that there is "plenty good enough material for a republic in the most degraded people that ever existed," Hank sets to work undermining the feudal order (*CY* 182). He has Arthur's knights sell toothbrushes and hats, organizes a stock market so that ambitious aristocrats may exhaust their desire for domination, and makes a fool of Merlin by dynamiting his tower. He even takes a crack at the established Church by fixing the leak in a "miraculously" dry holy well. To prepare the citizenry for republican government, he sets up "man factories," where promising young people are taught to read, write, and think for themselves. Religious diversity is encouraged, a network of telegraph cables is strung, and the implements of modern warfare are stockpiled, all to ensure the victory of the republican forces when Arthur dies.

We cannot fault Hank for his overall plan to democratize England, nor can we question his devotion to democracy. Although he becomes quite fond of power—especially of being called "The Boss"—Hank remains a fairly sympathetic character. At the least, his analysis of Camelot's vices seems to be a close approximation of what Twain himself would say, and his commitment to equality and progress is basically genuine.

Where Hank errs is in assuming that modern technological knowledge can bring about the sort of revolution he desires. After his adventure is over, Hank recounts how he had been a man "nearly barren of sentiment . . . or poetry" (*CY* 4), a fact that caused him to undertake reform in an overly clinical manner. Instead of inflaming the masses with populist rhetoric, he straightens the roads, teaches the Three R's, and embarks on a cleanliness crusade. While his basic insight is sound—that people must first be prepared for self-rule—the changes he seeks are superficial, like paint on a rotted fence. Hank encounters a similar problem when he tries to disguise King Arthur as a peasant: try as he might to hide Arthur's inner nobility, Hank cannot keep the king's character from shining through his rags. In both cases Hank focuses on the outward manifestations of subservience or assertiveness, rather than the core emotions that drive those behaviors. He reforms Camelot as a medical doctor would treat a patient: by observing, probing, dissecting, applying remedies proven in other cases. However, nei-

ther Hank nor the doctor sees his respective patient holistically or philosophically. Were Hank to do so, he would see that the feudal hierarchy of
Camelot, sustained by the Church, provides something to the masses that
they cannot get from Hank's version of democracy.[5] It may be fear that
drives Arthur's people into the Church's fold after the interdict, but that
fear is counterbalanced by a confidence in the Church's (and the feudal order's) ability to make sense of and allay that fear. The divine right of kings
may be a sham, but it is a sham that has penetrated to the soul of the
Camelotians, and straighter roads and newspapers are not going to sway
their allegiance when called upon to choose sides. Hank must provide a vision for society—this time not a sham one, rooted in primal fear—that
will touch people's souls and firmly commit them to revolutionary change.
Without this, people will only change their superficial behavior, as when a
new lord comes into power and has different ideas for how subjects should
behave. Sadly, Hank never fully understands Camelot philosophically until too late. The reforms he does achieve are due as much to his intimidating presence as The Boss as to any widespread acceptance of his republican
ideals. He does not convert the nation of worms back into a nation of men,
but merely puts himself in charge. By the time he realizes that he and his
reforms are devoid of sentiment and poetry, he reawakens in the nineteenth
century.

Henry Nash Smith has argued that *Connecticut Yankee* is a "fable of progress," juxtaposing outmoded forms of society and economy with America's
nascent industrial democracy, while Louis Budd and Howard Baetzhold
have demonstrated links between Twain's attitudes and contemporary social issues in Britain. All three, however, miss the broader significance of
the book as a critical reflection upon issues of hierarchy, submission, and
the exercise of liberty. Andrew Hoffman realizes this in part, when he argues that Twain draws a parallel in *Connecticut Yankee* between Camelot's
peasants and the sharecroppers and industrial workers of post–Civil War
America.[6] However, while it is true that severe economic inequality was
prevalent during the Gilded Age, and blue-collar workers had few rights,

5. On these points, see Wilson Carey McWilliams, *The Idea of Fraternity in America,* 460.
6. Henry Nash Smith, *Mark Twain's Fable of Progress;* Louis Budd, *Mark Twain: Social
Philosopher;* Howard Baetzhold, *Mark Twain and John Bull;* Andrew Hoffman, *Twain's Heroes, Twain's Worlds,* 132–35.

Twain's point is that medieval "freemen" did not exhibit the spirit of freedom. Though physically free, their souls were chained. It would be difficult to prove that American sharecroppers and factory workers lacked the spirit of freedom. Their situation was the reverse of Camelot's freemen: they were free in spirit but physically chained (by severe socioeconomic inequalities).

Fortunately for Americans, most of the hierarchical institutions of the Old World failed to make the voyage to the New World. This is not to say that formal hierarchies have not been an integral part of the development of the United States: slavery and the subordination of women are two glaring examples. Yet even these unjust, degrading institutions failed to effect the same sort of control as the Church and aristocracy did in Twain's Camelot. Despite being subjected to the sort of demeaning treatment that cramps the mind and stifles ambition, most American women and slaves were conscious of their equal worth long before the institutions depriving them of their equality were abolished—in large part because the egalitarian principles of the Declaration of Independence came to be seen as trumping (at least in a moral sense) inegalitarian laws. American institutions that preserve inequality have usually been viewed with skepticism—if not by everyone, then at least by committed minorities of the populace. Egalitarian sentiment has rarely been lacking in American history, which has minimized the danger of returning to the sort of hierarchical control found in Camelot. Yet this same egalitarianism presents its own problems.

The unifying theme of *Connecticut Yankee,* as I have interpreted it, concerns how abolishing the physical and legal institutions of hierarchical control is only the first step toward achieving the individual liberation necessary for democratic self-rule. Unless citizens' core convictions change, even the most liberal and just reforms will likely fail, prompting critics to conclude—incorrectly, but understandably—that democracy itself is to blame. If such a democracy continues to survive, individual development will probably be sluggish, if present at all. This is what the aesthetic critics see in America: a nation that purports to provide liberty, but in fact subjugates individuals to a tyrannical majority.

Since a democratic majority enjoys moral as well as physical authority, Tocqueville argues, it tends to extend its influence beyond the political arena to the realm of thought itself. When it has pronounced on an issue—

whether political or otherwise—citizens "make for the bandwagon." In such a society, people mistakenly believe that democratic equality implies identity or conformity, when it more properly should refer to the equal dignity or individuality of each person. Tocqueville remarks that although America is the most democratic nation on earth, there is "no country in which, speaking generally, there is less independence of mind and true freedom of discussion." Committed as they are to majority rule, Americans risk losing their status as individuals—and without respect for individuals, republican government is no better than common tyranny.[7] Twain's reminder that even egalitarian institutions require genuine independence of mind and spirit to flourish is the most powerful message of *Connecticut Yankee*.[8]

I will return to Twain later in the chapter, since his *Huckleberry Finn* centers around the *process* of liberation, but first we must focus more particularly on the nature of conformity within democracy, a favorite subject of Cooper's.

Giants and Pigmies: Egalitarianism in Cooper's New England

In his Littlepage Trilogy (*Satanstoe, The Chainbearer,* and *The Redskins*), James Fenimore Cooper challenges the common view that New England is a model for American democracy. To him, the form of democracy that flourishes in New England, while remarkable for its egalitarianism and high levels of civic involvement, nonetheless lacks true freedom of thought. Rather than being signs of moral courage and intrepidity, he argues, the strong beliefs of New Englanders are too often merely impressed upon citizens by their community. Through the character of Jason Newcome, Cooper demonstrates how the egalitarian conformity of New England democracy stifles individual development just as effectively as—sometimes more effectively than—the feudal hierarchy Twain satirizes in *Connecticut Yankee*.

7. Tocqueville, *Democracy,* 254–56.

8. As Alexander Saxton notes, Twain believed the evils accompanying the industrial revolution "were not inherent in technological progress, nor even in industrial capitalism. Rather they were to be seen as recurrences of mankind's ancient subservience to evil tricksters and self-serving imposters." Saxton, *The Rise and Fall of the White Republic,* 354. I would add that for Twain, tricksters and imposters need not be individual persons. *Huckleberry Finn,* for example, deals with tricksterism at both individual and cultural levels.

Early in the trilogy, Jason becomes the agent of the Littlepage family, who are establishing a town on the New York frontier. In the family's absence, however, Jason lines his pockets and undermines the Littlepages' authority through a variety of "law honest" but underhanded tricks. His manipulations, continued by his children and grandchildren, culminate in a violent rebellion against the legitimate rule of the Littlepages, an event that illustrates for Cooper the two troubling tendencies of New England–style democracy: its reliance on habitual conformity and its encouragement of demagoguery.

The son of a farmer, Jason had received no formal religious training. However, as Corny Littlepage, the narrator of *Satanstoe,* tells us, from an early age Jason had been expected to absorb not only the scriptures, but also numerous books of sermons, moral polemics, and essays on the supremacy of New England. Jason had discovered that all his actions and words were subject to the approval of his community's religious elders, and had learned to live under a highly restrictive code of conduct. When placed in a situation where he could enjoy what others consider harmless pleasures, he feels strangely guilty—prompting Corny to remark that Jason is constrained by his community like "a giant held in bondage by a pigmy" (*ST* 262–64).

Throughout *Satanstoe* we see the effects of Jason's Puritan upbringing. As he accompanies Corny to the frontier settlement at Ravensnest, Jason continually asks prying questions, extols the virtues of New England at every chance, and justifies his frequent sips of alcohol on medicinal grounds. He instinctively acts as if his "neighbors" were watching his every move. Even in the wilderness, Jason feels the community at his back; when Corny discovers him playing cards with an Episcopal minister, Jason quickly hides the deck under his leg. His visible embarrassment at having been "convicted of being engaged in the damning sin of handling certain spotted pieces of paper, invented for, and used in the combination of a game played for amusement" delights Corny immensely (*ST* 402–3).

Jason's conduct, though comical, is illustrative of a deeper character flaw. It is one thing to believe that card playing and drinking are wrong, or that Connecticut is the best place on earth, but Jason is able to justify those beliefs only with reference to the authority of his community. He has received his convictions as a child would—accepting them as correct without an explanation. Although Puritan leaders could probably provide thoughtful arguments against both drinking and card playing, the nature of Puritan education prevented Jason from learning and *thoughtfully* accepting these justifications. To him, playing with pieces of spotted paper was a sin because from birth his community and its elders had told him it was—just as they had told him drinking was wrong, and that the New England way of life was superior to all others.

Cooper believed this way of thinking to be doubly dangerous. The first danger is that people like Jason live as mere instruments of their community, receiving and acting upon its ideas of right or wrong, without a moment's reflection. Yankee stubbornness, in this view, is less a symbol of independence than of enthusiasm for one's indoctrinated habits. Even the famed Yankee ingenuity could be seen (as in the aesthetic critics' eyes) as faithful adherence to an unquestioned cult of practicality and "usefulness." Jason and those like him are assets to no society, such as liberal democracy, that values individuality and free choice.

The second danger is that once someone leaves such a controlling community, he will begin to view the code of conduct as mere arbitrary convention not deserving of continued allegiance. In *Satanstoe* Jason discovers that not all communities are as strict as his own, and that his new friends care little if he indulges moderately in drink and sport. This leads him to doubt whether his Puritan code is based on anything more universal than a community's whim. Having resolved that certain sins are arbitrarily defined, he glides to the conclusion that all communal proscriptions are arbitrary. Having renounced the overall legitimacy of the code, he is free to ignore those elements that run counter to his inclinations, and, in Machiavellian fashion, to conform to the remainder when they advance his interests. To Cooper, this tendency toward ethical nihilism (the rejection of all customary beliefs) is just as dangerous to democracy as the "giant held in bondage by a pigmy" problem. At best, the nihilist will not care to develop his abilities, thinking all knowledge and norms are suspect from the start. At worst, he will endanger the very democratic forms that provide space for his skeptical questioning; he will come to see democracy as a power relationship that sacrifices the strong to the weak. Since the nihilist rejects any belief in natural equality—one of the tenets of the old "arbitrary" code—as a matter of course he discards democracy as well. Whereas in the first case democracy is incompletely realized, in this case it becomes the plaything of ambitious, unprincipled demagogues. Either way, democracy is put in harm's way.

At the beginning of the trilogy, Jason's behavior demonstrates the first danger: being unable to defend his beliefs thoughtfully and courageously. As the trilogy progresses, however, he steadily emancipates himself from the restrictive code of his youth. Living in the wilderness, he finds he can safely ignore the Puritan prohibitions against lying, cheating, and extravagant living, as long as he does not *appear* to be violating them. After all, in his eyes each prohibition is merely a convention. After stripping away layers of Puritan restrictions on behavior, what remains is an exhortation to worldly success, Calvinist evidence of one's state of grace.[9] Jason was brought up to believe that although resources should not be enjoyed lavishly, wealth was desirable, and in fact would signify his worth. This code was ingrained in him; no deliberation had taken place on his part. When Jason leaves for the wilderness of New York, traditional restrictions on the use of money begin to seem as arbitrary as prohibitions on drinking or card playing. However, since this part of the code hardly conflicts with his selfish desires, he does not bother to discard it. Free from communal oversight and "conventions," Jason relentlessly pursues his own self-interest, twisting the law and flattering the people.

Jason's nihilism—the result of breaking free from a community that overly indoctrinates its citizens—gives him an advantage over the other New Englanders at Ravensnest, who still believe in the old code. He knows exactly how to manipulate them, since they are unable to resist demagogues when separated from their paternalistic leaders. In *The Chainbearer,* we find Jason presiding over a town meeting convened to choose a denomination for the new church building at Ravensnest. A bare plurality of the assembly favors Congregationalism, while the rest favor other sects. Jason employs a series of procedural tricks to ensure a Congregational majority (for example, after each ballot the denomination gathering the fewest votes is dropped from the next ballot), but a close win is not enough to satisfy him.

9. As Max Weber notes, the Puritan sects, unlike medieval guilds, were "devoid of the purpose of a material subsistence policy which handicapped an expansion of the rational striving for profit." In fact, "the capitalist success of a sect brother, if legally attained, was proof of his worth and of his state of grace." Weber, "The Protestant Sects and the Spirit of Capitalism," in *From Max Weber,* 322.

A clever demagogue, he knows an even larger victory is within reach. Playing on the indoctrinated religious and political convictions of the townsfolk, a great number of whom are native Yankees, Jason exhorts the assembly to support his denomination unanimously: "Fellow-citizens, we have been dealing with the most important interest that consarns man; his religious state, government, and well-being. Unanimity is very desirable on such a question; and as it is to be presumed no one will oppose the pop'lar will, I shall now put the question to vote for the purpose of obtaining that unanimity. Those who are in favor of the Congregationals, or who ardently wish that denomination, will hold up their hands." Immediately three-fourths of the hands go up; when the people start shouting "unanimity, unanimity," many more are raised. Mordaunt Littlepage, the narrator of *The Chainbearer*, observes, "The moderator and two or three of his friends made short speeches, commending the liberality of a part of the citizens, and congratulating all, when the meeting was adjourned" (*CB* 292).

Cooper's critique of New England may seem odd at first, and it is likely overstated (given Cooper's strong attachment to New York), but in this episode he accurately identifies the dangerous tendencies of New England–style democracy. Ever concerned that foreign critics would mistake problems on the surface of America for problems with core American values, Cooper seeks to refocus our attention on the Middle Atlantic states, where adherence to equality is tempered and sustained by a genuine love of individual liberty. Only where democracy is joined with liberalism, he implies, will people be able to rise above paternalistic control, resist the flattery of demagogues, and begin to shape the world for themselves.

Natty Bumppo and the Promise of Democratic Liberation

For the novelists, in particular Cooper, understanding democracy's potential requires examining democratic man apart from the complications of imposed communal obligations. Natty Bumppo of Cooper's Leatherstocking Tales, a man of the wilderness with only a smattering of formal education, is an excellent candidate for this investigation.

Natty appears in *The Deerslayer*[10] as a young man renowned for his hunt-

10. The Leatherstocking Tales were written out of order, with *The Deerslayer* (which de-

ing abilities. As the book opens, Natty and "Hurry Harry" March arrive at Glimmerglass Lake, where they meet Tom Hutter, a local trapper, and Chingachgook, Natty's Delaware friend. Having discovered that a band of French-allied Hurons is nearby, Hutter and Harry—against Natty's counsel (discussed in Chapter 4)—embark upon a nighttime scalp raid, thus beginning the escalating cycle of struggle, capture, and escape that serves as backdrop for Cooper's investigation into human nature.

Natty is, in many respects, the epitome of natural man.[11] He loves honesty, justice, and wisdom genuinely, not from social conditioning. Whereas Hutter and Hurry Harry are driven by greed, which is encouraged not so much by nature as by the colonial government's scalp bounties, Natty is reluctant to commit violence. Having never been taught to view other races as anything but equals, Natty sees horrid injustice in killing simply for money. When the Hurons scalp, he notes, they at least do it for honor (*DS* 42–44). Although he identifies with the white race, he sees it as but one small part of humanity. His refusal to treat Native Americans as inferiors is exhibited in his friendship with Chingachgook and his refusal to return fire before a Huron adversary can reload (*DS* 59–63). He admits that he can be a little too trusting of others, but he prefers to err in that direction than to adopt the attitude of Hutter and Harry.

Natty's relative isolation from communal norms does not reduce him to barbarism. In fact, it is Hurry Harry whom Cooper terms a "handsome barbarian." Harry enjoys good looks, the physique of a giant, and a boisterous sense of humor—all of which contribute to his handsomeness. However, his barbarism is rooted in his arrogant outlook toward the world, shaped by his upbringing as a white man in the settlements. He exhibits his utter callousness at one point when, on a whim, he shoots at a Huron girl from Hutter's boat. Chingachgook's fiancée Hist furiously berates Harry for his heartless act; the following passage records Harry's response:

---

picts Natty in his youth) finished last, in 1841. Next in the sequence is *The Last of the Mohicans* (1826), followed by *The Pathfinder* (1840), *The Pioneers* (1823), and *The Prairie* (1827). Each book covers a different period in Natty's life, with *The Pioneers* and *The Prairie* depicting his old age and death.

11. R. W. B. Lewis calls him "the full-fledged fictional Adam" in *The American Adam*, 104. Lawrence Buell, in the introduction to *The Environmental Imagination*, cautions against the use of this image, with its masculine biases. A more comprehensive account of Natty Bumppo would address, of course, Buell's concern in depth; given the brevity of my discussion, I can only mention it before continuing onward.

Like most vulgar-minded men . . . [i]t had never struck him that the affections are human; that even high principles—modified by habits and prejudices, but not the less elevated within their circle—can exist in the savage state; and that the warrior who is most ruthless in the field can submit to the softest and gentlest influences in the moments of domestic quiet. In a word, it was the habit of his mind to regard all Indians as being only a slight degree removed from the wild beasts that roamed the woods, and to feel disposed to treat them accordingly. . . . Still, though daunted by these reproaches, the handsome barbarian could hardly be said to be penitent. . . . Instead of resenting, or answering the simple but natural appeal of Hist, he walked away like one who disdained entering into a controversy with a woman. (*DS* 170–71)

Harry views Native Americans as a typical settler would. Although he possesses a strong independent streak and a well-developed antipathy toward law and order, he is still a creation of his community (the frontier settlements). Paradoxically, even his brazen independence and aversion to established law were instilled in him by his rough-and-tumble community. To borderers like Harry, Indians had always been, at best, enemies to fight and defeat, and at worst an infestation of pests that need exterminating. Either way, the settlers' view is biased in a way that prevents the peaceful resolution of the racial conflict. It is based in large part upon irrational notions and fears, and because it is deeply ingrained in the community's set of beliefs it is quite resistant to change. Even rational persuasion makes slow headway against such a deeply held conviction.

Because his only community, in any tangible sense, consists of the Moravian missionaries who taught him patience and tolerance as a boy, Natty is abler than Harry to see beyond the prejudices of his race. He is quick to praise the virtues of the Delawares, and even recognizes that the Hurons are not purely evil beings. Although he realizes there are good reasons for fighting the Hurons, he notes that even his sworn enemies are humans like himself, and worthy of his respect.

Natty is subject neither to a hierarchy nor to the whims of his neighbors; he is his own man, and any obligations he accepts are for the most part grounded in his consent. He is able to live according to his "gifts," and can become the sort of person he is best suited to be—in his case a hunter and scout. He is free to develop his natural talents, unlike Twain's Arthurian peasants and Cooper's New Englanders. Of course, his opportunities for development are somewhat limited in the middle of a forest. If he had a "gift" for being a merchant, for example, he could not choose to be one in the backwoods. However, the issue of opportunity is separate from that of freedom. Liberal democracy promises a great deal of freedom to choose one's ends, but it does not make all ends feasible. Natty can grow as a person within the constraints of his environment—not just those of his imagination.

The fact that liberal democracy removes barriers to enable fuller individual development helps vindicate the ideal of democratic freedom against the aesthetic critique. Cooper may indeed romanticize Natty, but he does so to demonstrate that we cannot gauge the true potential of democracy simply by observing its actual practice. He himself feared American democracy would fall prey to majoritarian conformity, but he remained confident that democracy, properly understood, could elevate everyone's lives. Natty serves, then, as a model for American democrats, for by emulating his free mind and spirit, we can pull ourselves out of the equality of similarity into the equality of independent individuals. We need not live in the woods like Natty, but we should think and act more like him within the confines of our daily lives.[12] Natty's independence—his ability to define himself as more than a part of a hierarchy or community—is perfectly consistent with being a farmer, businessperson, household manager, or scholar. It is not, however, equivalent to Jason Newcome's independence. Both Jason and Natty tend to reject conventions, but Jason does so because the conventions do not serve his interest. Natty, however, opposes only those laws that contradict nature and reason.

Cooper's concern was that Americans will not live up to the promise of democracy; he intended Natty Bumppo to inspire readers to transcend the hierarchical and communal bonds that stifle original thinking. Democratic institutions can remove many of these fetters, by protecting individual rights and freedom of speech. However, unless the democratic spirit of liberty is extended to those relationships commonly considered nonpolitical, individual development will still be hindered. Cooper was appalled by the

12. On Natty as model, see Catherine H. Zuckert, *Natural Right and the American Imagination*, 5, chap. 2.

utter subjection of women in frontier families,[13] and distressed at the impulse toward conformity among Americans in general, all of which takes place within liberal political institutions. Kay Seymour House notes that Natty's innocence "is properly opposed to the rote learning in schools of the mistaken notions in a narrow education, to the institutionalized religion that puts cant between man and God, to speculation and a priori decisions that deny experiential truths, to anything—in short—that keeps a man from examining, with every means he has, life itself." As long as people are subject to the constraints of hierarchy and conformity in their daily lives, formal political freedom will contribute little to individual development. Development can occur only if the spirit of democracy extends beyond strictly political institutions to the culture of everyday life.[14]

Huckleberry Finn and the Process of Liberation

Cooper treats Natty Bumppo as something of an ideal democrat, intuiting justice without being overawed by a community's will, but even Cooper realizes that Natty's life is in tension with the demands of ordinary civilized society. Human nature being what it is—a mix of good and evil—Natty seems superhuman. Huckleberry Finn, in comparison, hardly seems to be an exemplary character. Son of the town drunk, he dresses in rags, lives in a hogshead, and prides himself on his wart-curing abilities. Twain's use of an outcast in condemning the social norms of the Old South forcefully demonstrates the importance of democratic liberation to individual development. By running away from home and experiencing the world for himself, Huck comes to realize the truth about his society. Liberation elevates his character, and he becomes able to think for himself. *Adventures of Huckleberry Finn* confirms Cooper's view that democratic freedom must extend beyond formal institutions to citizens' daily lives, if individual development is to occur.

13. Cooper's depictions of Esther Bush in *The Prairie* and Prudence Thousandacres in *The Chainbearer* illustrate the tragedy of capable, heroic women being subjected to tyrannical husbands.

14. Kay Seymour House, *Cooper's Americans,* 288. For an interpretation that emphasizes how Natty Bumppo embodies the virtues of an older civilization that "must be superseded," see John P. McWilliams Jr., *Political Justice in a Republic,* 129.

Huck illustrates the overwhelming pressure toward conformity that society often places upon its members (even those on its fringes) and the difficulty in establishing oneself as a thinking, self-determining individual. Although Huck stubbornly resists the "sivilizing" influences of the Widow
Douglas and Miss Watson, his community's norms nonetheless do constrain him. Only by helping Jim, Miss Watson's slave, escape down the Mississippi River does he begin to view those norms critically. As he agonizes
over whether to follow his conscience (programmed by his community to
consider slavery a positive good) and turn Jim in to the authorities, or to
remain loyal to his friend (and receive eternal damnation), he becomes
more than a member of a community. He rises to his full height—or at
least substantially higher than he had been before.

After staging his own death and setting off down the river, Huck discovers Jim has also escaped. Though his "conscience" tells him to turn Jim
in, to avoid being labeled a "low down Ablitionist," Huck knows it would
be awkward to return to town after being dead. So he and Jim continue
down the river. At this point Jim is hardly Huck's *friend,* since Huck knows
him only as a harmless, superstitious fellow he and Tom Sawyer used to tor-
ment. Jim is just a slave, nothing more. When he tells of his plan to smug-
gle his wife and children out of slavery, Huck is appalled. He wonders what
the owners of Jim's family had done to deserve such ungrateful treatment
(*HF* 69, 123–24).

Even if, as Leo Marx argues, Huck's instinctive humanity shows through
while he is still on Jackson Island with Jim,[15] it is nonetheless clear that
Huck does not treat Jim as a full friend. Although he grew up on the edge
of society, Huck has fully internalized his community's norms; his conscience tells him slavery is good and just, and must be maintained. As he
tells the reader, "My conscience got to stirring me up hotter than ever, until at last I says to it, 'Let up on me—it ain't too late, yet—I'll paddle ashore
at the first light, and tell.'" As soon as he decides to rat on Jim, he "felt easy,
and happy, and light as a feather, right off" (*HF* 124).

When Huck shoves off for shore, though, Jim yells out: "Jim won't ever
forget you, Huck; you's de bes' fren' Jim's ever had; en you's de *only* fren' old

---

15. Leo Marx, "Mr. Eliot, Mr. Trilling, and *Huckleberry Finn,*" in Harold Bloom, ed.,
Mark Twain's Adventures of Huckleberry Finn, 9.

Jim's got now." Huck, who had been "all in a sweat" to tell on Jim, stops paddling; until now he had been sure of his actions. But Jim's words, Huck relates, "seemed to kind of take the tuck all out of me." As Huck continues on, Jim yells, "Dah you goes, de ole true Huck; de on'y white genlman dat ever kep' his promise to ole Jim." Now Huck begins to feel queasy—but does not recognize his sick feelings as a sign of his true conscience kicking in. On the contrary, he tells himself, "I *got* to do it—I can't get *out* of it." Conscience—or at least what he perceives to be his conscience—dictates that he hold steady to his course (*HF* 124–25).

When Huck lies to two slave hunters to save Jim, he feels remorse, and despairs of ever possessing enough courage to follow his conscience. He still does not recognize that his supposed lack of fortitude is due in fact to the workings of his genuine conscience, which has been awakened by his growing friendship with Jim (*HF* 127–28). His reflections upon his supposed moral failure are worth noting: "I thought a minute, and says to myself, hold on,—s pose you'd a done right and give Jim up; would you felt better than what you do now? No, says I, I'd feel bad—I'd feel just the same way I do now. Well, then, says I, what's the use you learning to do right, when it's troublesome to do right and ain't no trouble to do wrong, and the wages is just the same? I was struck. I couldn't answer that. So I reckoned I wouldn't bother no more about it, but after this always do whichever come handiest at the time." For Huck it is still not a question of whether his community's standards are right or wrong, but whether he can live up to them. However, by questioning the utility of doing right, Huck begins to see beyond the limits of his community's imagination. If doing "wrong" is easier than doing "right," he notes, and if the consequences are the same, then why should anyone bother doing what is right? As Huck considers this question, he begins to see how slavery lacks justification. His reasoning may be crude, but it at least enables him to see the institution from a different perspective. It is significant that at this point Huck takes the money the slave hunters had given him and splits it equally with Jim (*HF* 128).

When con men sell Jim back into slavery, Huck sits alone on the raft and ponders his next move. Overwhelmed by his guilt for helping Jim, and knowing that "it would be a thousand times better for Jim to be a slave at home where his family was, as long as he'd *got* to be a slave," he considers writing a letter to Miss Watson, notifying her of Jim's location. At first he hesitates, fearing he will become a social pariah if word gets out that he helped a slave escape. But then he castigates himself for having second thoughts:

> That's just the way: a person does a low-down thing, and then he don't want to take no consequences of it. Thinks as long as he can hide it, it ain't no disgrace. That was my fix exactly. The more I studied about this, the more my conscience went to grinding me, and the more wicked and low-down and ornery I got to feeling. And at last, when it hit me all of a sudden that here was the plain hand of Providence slapping me in the face and letting me know my wickedness was being watched all the time from up there in heaven . . . I most dropped in my tracks I was so scared.

Huck's fear drives him to draft a note to Miss Watson. Knowing he can now pray for forgiveness, he sets it aside for a moment. But instead of praying, he tells the reader that he

> got to thinking over our trip down the river; and I see Jim before me, all the time, in the day, and in the nighttime, sometimes moonlight, sometimes storms, and we a floating along, talking, and singing, and laughing. But somehow I couldn't seem to strike no places to harden me against him, but only the other kind. I'd see him standing my watch on top of his'n, stead of calling me, so I could go on sleeping; and see him how glad he was when I come back out of the fog . . . and at last I struck the time I saved him by telling the [slave hunters] we had small-pox aboard, and he was so grateful, and said I was the best friend old Jim ever had in the world, and the *only* one he's got now.

Huck rips up the note, confident that although his actions are wrong by the community's standards, he has no alternative. While he reasons that his failure to defend slavery is due to a lack of good training (he blames his wickedness on his upbringing), his reluctance to turn Jim in actually stems from his developing, though still not fully recognized, friendship with Jim. Swearing, "All right, then, I'll *go* to hell," he vows to steal Jim out of slavery (*HF* 269–72).

Huck finds the Phelps farm, where Jim is being held. By a stroke of luck, the Phelpses are Tom Sawyer's kin, and Tom happens to show up just after Huck arrives. The boys discover Jim in a rickety shed behind the house, and Tom vows to help rescue him. Huck's plan to break Jim out in the middle of the night is straightforward and workable, but Tom argues it is "too blame' simple; there ain't nothing *to* it. . . . it wouldn't make no more talk than breaking into a soap factory" (*HF* 294). Tom, reflecting the norms of his society, devises an elaborate "evasion," full of danger and romance but devoid of reason. Instead of sneaking out the shed's window or being let out by the boys, Jim is to remain in his cell for weeks, writing cryptic messages in blood and fabricating ropes out of bed sheets. Meanwhile, Tom and Huck are to dig under the foundation of the shed with case knives, consistent with all the "authorities" on great escapes. To increase the danger, Tom sends a note to the Phelpses, warning them that robbers plan to steal Jim during the night. The Phelpses naturally gather a band of armed men, who shoot Tom in the leg during the night escape.

Even when faint from blood loss, Tom remains in his imaginary world—like everyone else in southern aristocratic society. When the trio reach the raft, Tom exhorts his companions to make good their escape:

> "Don't stop now; don't fool around here, and the evasion booming along so handsome; man the sweeps, and set her loose! Boys, we done it elegant!—'deed we did. I wish *we'd* a had the handling of Louis XVI., there wouldn't a been no 'Son of Saint Louis, ascend to heaven!' wrote in *his* biography: no, sir, we'd a whooped him over the *border*—that's what we'd a done with *him*—and done it just as slick as nothing at all, too. Man the sweeps—man the sweeps!" (*HF* 344)

Fortunately, both Jim and Huck are more levelheaded than Tom. Though he knows he will be returned to slavery as a result, Jim insists they fetch a doctor. And sure enough, Tom is put to bed and Jim is clapped in irons.

It is then that Tom reveals that Jim has been a free man all along; Miss Watson had died and manumitted him in her will. The fact that Tom knew this but did not tell anyone, least of all Huck and Jim, speaks to the utter senselessness of his guiding principles. For Tom, freeing Jim was a game—just like the robber gang Tom had founded at the beginning of the book. Jim was simply an object of entertainment, someone on whom to play practical jokes or with whom to swap stories and superstitions.

Huck, on the other hand, sees Jim in a different light. He has come to consider Jim as something approaching a friend: in other words, someone to confide in, treat as an equal, and protect. By the end of the novel, he may not have completely discarded his society's norms (after all, he has resigned himself to a life of wickedness), but he has gone a long way toward rejecting the institution of slavery. Unlike Tom, whose "drive to dominate his companions ⁞ . . . arises from the imitative aspect of his mind," Huck "reacts sensitively to life about him . . . invest[ing] the objects and people of his world with a life of their own."[16] His budding friendship with Jim gives him the beginnings of a true understanding of southern hierarchy: namely, that it is founded on dreams and fantasies. In this sense, Huck's journey down the river has been liberating. He can now see his society with a clearer, more objective eye. He is becoming his own man, able to judge for himself which standards of behavior are appropriate. Whereas before he was an outcast in name, but a devotee to communal norms regarding slavery in fact, he has now gained critical distance from his society, and knows that "sivilization" is not always consistent with democracy. Richard P. Adams shrewdly notes that Huck's moral dilemma is significantly more complex than Thoreau's in *Civil Disobedience*. According to Adams, Thoreau "feels himself on solid ground when his conscience tells him to oppose the extension of slavery and the government that sanctions and promotes it," whereas Huck does right only by "doing what he thoroughly believes, in his conscious mind, to be wrong." This is what makes Huck truly admirable and, I would add, what makes him a realistic and plausible character.[17]

Huck's newfound independence fulfills the promise of liberal democracy, which seeks to free individuals from both hierarchy and the egalitarian pressure toward conformity. However, this liberation is not to be absolute, like Natty Bumppo's freedom. Rather, democratic institutions carve out a space for individuals *within* society, enabling citizens to choose their own

16. James M. Cox, "Remarks on the Sad Initiation of Huckleberry Finn," in Barry A. Marks, ed., *Mark Twain's Huckleberry Finn*, 70. McWilliams, while not seeing much actual transformation in Huck's outlook, believes that *Huckleberry Finn* "suggest[s] a better road for the American," free from the "follies of regality." See McWilliams, *Idea of Fraternity*, 464–65.

17. Richard P. Adams, "The Unity and Coherence of *Huckleberry Finn*," in Marks, ed., *Mark Twain's Huckleberry Finn*, 86–87.

courses of action and to accept only those restrictions to which they have consented. Because they can now see the world for themselves, and are left to shape their own life plans, they can rise to their full height. Their minds and hearts are not simply extensions of their community, but are their own; they can be committed to beliefs freely, without compulsion. They may pursue their tastes and develop their talents as they wish, a key precondition for the fuller development of their abilities.

Silas Lapham's Fall and Rise

Like Twain, Howells is concerned with liberation from unreasonable social norms, but in a context that more closely resembles modern urban industrial society. In *The Rise of Silas Lapham,* Howells tells of a classic self-made man, the son of a Vermont farmer who makes a fortune in the mineral paint business—thanks to dedication, hard work, and a mine of top-quality ingredients his father had discovered. Silas Lapham moves his family to Boston, where they attempt to enter the established circle of Beacon Hill aristocrats. At first the Brahmins reject him as a mere money-loving clod with no sense for the finer things in life. However, over time Silas comes to realize his own narrowness and begins to consider the social effects of his self-interested actions. After a series of embarrassments and the loss of his fortune, he frees himself from the hard-nosed capitalist ethics endorsed by bourgeois society and returns to Vermont a better man.

What makes *Silas Lapham* unique, compared to other Victorian novels of industrial society, is the way Howells frames the problem. Whereas Charles Dickens and Elizabeth Gaskell examine the bourgeois mentality in the context of uneasy relations between employers and laborers, thereby emphasizing how capitalist ethics exacerbate social division, Howells focuses on how the capitalist becomes degraded even during times of peaceful employer-employee relations. Silas Lapham is a commendable employer, keeping his factories open until the very end, and doing nothing to provoke his workers to strike. His industrial management is a model of humane efficiency. However, despite his sense of justice and duty, there is still something missing in his character—something that can be seen most clearly in the context of satisfactory industrial relations, where questions of distributive justice and duty are less salient. Howells certainly appreciated the injustice of many existing social arrangements (*A Hazard of New Fortunes,* for example, is set in the midst of a violent streetcar-workers' strike), but justice was not his only concern. In *Silas Lapham* he purposefully sets aside many key questions of social justice in order to isolate the effects of bourgeois society on Silas's development as an individual.

The book opens with a reporter interviewing Silas for a newspaper article headlined "Solid Men of Boston." Silas tells of his rural upbringing, traditional education, and devoted parents—old hat to the reporter, who had already interviewed a number of similar men. In his mind, all risen Americans have gone through a period in which they are all "pathetically alike in their narrow circumstances, their sufferings, and their aspirations." When Silas begins to ramble on about his mother and life on the homestead, the reporter begins to yawn (*SL* 5–6).

However, the parts of the interview that bore the reporter are most revealing of Silas's character. We find, for instance, that Silas is deeply reverent toward his parents; he notes that his mother tirelessly cared for six boys while his rheumatic father worked from dawn to dusk in the fields. When his father failed to capitalize on the paint mine's potential and his brothers left home, Silas remained—and not, as one might think, because of the paint mine. He stayed behind, he tells the reporter, because of the old house and the graves of his family. Prior to his meteoric economic successes, in other words, Silas had been a decent, ordinary fellow. He had no strong desire for wealth and luxury, and was content with a moderate standard of living, achieved through honest dealing and hard work. When he discovers that paint made from the minerals on his farm is of higher quality than any other, he is overjoyed—not just because he will make a fortune, but because his product will be a "blessing to the world" (*SL* 17).

The fact that Silas was once such a man—and that even at the pinnacle of his success he expresses appreciation, not disdain, for his former life— is significant to Howells. It demonstrates that Silas can be redeemed. If he would only remove the blinders of capitalist self-interest and see the narrowness of his community's standard of excellence, the solid values of his youth could once again rise to the top of his character. He could become a better human being, seeing the true consequences of his actions and discovering the real meaning of his existence.

Silas's rise to fortune is fairly straightforward. After serving in the Civil

War, he takes on a partner with capital and begins to dominate the market with his high-quality paint. Before long he is able to move his wife, Persis, and daughters, Irene and Penelope, to Boston. He takes pride in the fact that the fires in his Vermont paint facilities have never gone out and that he has never cut his workers' wages. Business is booming beyond his wildest expectations.

However, he senses that wealth is not enough. He is not quite able to identify what is missing, what he is striving to attain, but he thinks he sees it in the Coreys, a Beacon Hill family. Although at times he considers the Coreys lazy, uninspired aristocrats, the life they lead has a certain appeal for him. Silas knows he lacks Bromfield Corey's cultivated taste and elegant manner, and is envious of his higher social status. He throws himself into his work, hoping to make enough money to establish his family (in particular his daughters) in high society. He tries his best to buy his way into the Brahmin circle, throwing away bundles of money on poorly chosen clothes, books, and a mansion on Beacon Hill. He believes that if he possesses all the trappings of an aristocrat, he will be treated as one. However, his fear of being excluded from society severely handicaps him when the Coreys invite the Laphams to dinner.

The dinner party scene illustrates two important miscalculations on Silas's part. First, he believes he can gain noble status by adhering to a particular code of conduct. This conception is attractive to a rich man such as himself, because nearly every social convention can be satisfied with sufficient funds. Thus Silas goes to great lengths to conform to the rules of Boston's genteel society, encasing his hands in ill-fitting, impractical gloves, drinking large quantities of wine, and telling stories that place himself in a good light. When he discovers he was a disgrace at the party, Silas abhors himself; his mea culpa in front of Bromfield's son, Tom, demonstrates his pathetic faith in the code of manners. In Silas's view, if only he could have better adhered to the proper standards of behavior, perhaps he would still have been able to associate with the Beacon Hill crowd. Blind to the fact that true nobility involves the cultivation of character, Silas attributes his supposed fall from respectability to an inability to conform to a code. In this he is greatly mistaken, as Howells demonstrates later in the work.

Silas's second error is to idolize the Coreys. Despite his contempt for Bromfield's idleness, he wishes to be like him: rich, refined, and well respected. What he misses is that only some elements of the Corey way of life are worth emulating. The norms of Silas's class dictate that Beacon Hill aristocrats deserve high respect, and he takes this to heart. However, to become just like the aristocrats would require giving up a certain natural vibrancy and sense of the world—qualities essential to a well-developed character, but lacking in Bromfield and other idle aristocrats. Silas fails to realize that the noble character he desires requires both the aristocrat's broader outlook and the energy of the democratic self-made man.

The two errors are related, and both are caused by Silas's indoctrination into a bourgeois view of the world. On the one hand, bourgeois society places great value on wealth and its ability to provide social status and material comfort for its possessor. Once an object of desire is chosen (for example, membership in Beacon Hill society), the means of achieving that object are obvious: buy it. Thus Silas uses his wealth to copy the forms of nobility, believing imitation is sufficient grounds for inclusion. But the bourgeois mentality does not give priority only to money as a means to an end. It also gives priority to certain ends—especially those that can be discussed in monetary terms, like the trappings of aristocracy. The bourgeoisie has difficulty seeing beyond the elements of aristocratic privilege that can be bought and sold (like dinner parties and dress gloves) to the real essence of nobility: the ability to orient one's life around higher pursuits, and to view wealth as, at best, an instrumental good.

Silas's community places a high value on being held in high esteem, which in itself is a laudable goal. However, Silas comes to emulate the Brahmins chiefly because his society deems them worthy of emulation. He models himself after the Beacon Hill circle in a characteristically bourgeois manner, emphasizing the aristocracy's outward forms and neglecting its driving spirit. His desire to become a gentleman is encouraged by society's norms, not personal reflection.

However, Silas's awkward forays into high society, coupled with increasingly dire prospects for his business, give him a new perspective on his system of values. He begins to realize that despite his conformity to the dictates of justice, he has become a narrow-minded man, incapable of appreciating human goods apart from their monetary value. Consequently, when given the opportunity to swindle a group of British investors, Silas refuses. Although this leads to the loss of his fortune, his principled actions in the

face of disaster earn him Beacon Hill's respect. He displays further nobility by turning down Tom Corey's offer of investment capital, knowing that
by accepting the money he would only be taking advantage of the young
man. Upon hearing this, Tom's uncle remarks that Silas "has behaved very
well—like a gentleman," that it is "hard to behave like a gentleman where
your interest is concerned," and that "[i]t must have cost him something
to say no to [Tom], for he's just in that state when he believes that this or
that chance, however small, would save him." Even Bromfield Corey was
able to find "a delicate, aesthetic pleasure in the heroism with which
Lapham had withstood [the] temptations,—something finely dramatic
and unconsciously effective" (*SL* 300, 359).

The Laphams sell their house and move back to Vermont, where Silas
reconciles himself to the fact that he will never live a triumphant life again.
However, everyone who knows his situation says he "behaved well, and
even more than well, when it came to the worst." Not only does he regain
the prudence and good sense he had "shown in the first years of his success,
and of which his great prosperity seemed to have bereft him," but his concern that "no one should suffer by him" gives his creditors confidence and
a lenient attitude toward his debts. Silas remains on good terms with his
new competitors; after all, "they had used him fairly; it was their facilities
that had conquered him, not their ill-will." Free from the suffocating, twisting norms of bourgeois society, Silas is once again guided by his innate
moral sense (*SL* 352–53).

Silas's regeneration is symbolized by the marriage of Penelope to Tom
Corey. Their union brings together the best of both worlds—the natural
spirit and energy of the Laphams and the broad-mindedness of the Coreys.
If only Silas had realized earlier the true value of the Coreys, instead of
merely mimicking their outward behavior, then perhaps he would not have
come to such an end. However, as soon as he moved to Boston and adopt-
ed society's skewed opinion of Beacon Hill, he was blinded to that value.
He did not realize that the Coreys could provide an important complement
(and corrective) to his common sense and narrow opinions. It is only after
he takes off the blinders imposed by his wealth- and status-addicted society that he can discover a truer relation between people and things, forti-
fying his earlier moral convictions while broadening his outlook. He now
knows that greatness of character is determined not simply by wealth, but

by the ability to rank material comfort appropriately in the scale of human goods.

Prior to his encounter with the Coreys, Silas—like millions of modern "self-made" people—lacks the necessary perspective to examine his own bourgeois values critically. Nevertheless, being confronted with values substantially at odds with his own (as Huck Finn is confronted by the fact of his friendship with Jim) dramatically changes his outlook on life. In the end he partially rejects the bourgeois code, having come to a better understanding of its relative importance. His ability to see social norms for what they are, and to scrutinize carefully those that seem to inhibit his development as an individual, is the mark of a true democratic person, free in spirit as well as body.

Cooper, Twain, and Howells all agree that democracy, more than any other regime, allows people to develop themselves as individuals. By replacing feudal hierarchy with political and legal equality, democracy provides room for citizens to pursue their talents and find their most suitable roles in life. The destruction of paternalistic institutions also means that individuals can (and in fact must) view their surroundings with their own eyes, not those of their social superiors. Knowledge gained in this way may require more individual effort, but has the advantage of being unmediated and unfiltered. Democrats are not utterly dependent on an outside authority for their beliefs; they are able to take a detached view of both nature and society, and can judge both more objectively. They become more fully human, in addition to becoming better citizens.

This, of course, is a somewhat idealized view of the effects of democratic liberation, but it makes clear the promise of democracy: to give ordinary people substantial power over their lives and communities.[18] It is the ideal embodied in Cooper's Natty Bumppo, the fiercely independent man of the wilderness, capable of ruling himself in isolation from all but the most rudimentary forms of society. It is an ideal in tension with certain traditional forms of community, to be sure, but it serves to remind us that democracy should imply liberty as well as equality. A democracy that ensures equal

18. For a magisterial history of this ideal in American life, see James E. Block, *A Nation of Agents*.

treatment of its citizens without giving room for independent thought and action only partially fulfills this promise.

This is the concern of both Twain and Cooper. Twain emphasizes that subjecting individuals to a higher human power—whether an individual or society—without justification leads to the shriveling of the soul, while Cooper points to the potential for nihilism and stark egoism among members of highly restrictive communities. By itself a democratic political regime may not be sufficient for preventing these problems; for unless the *spirit* of democratic liberty extends throughout civil society and the family, a community will be democratic in name only. Those critics who castigate democrats for their self-seeking, uncultured lifestyles are really only observing partially developed democrats. They see the American equivalent of Twain's peasants, unable to think for themselves and all too willing to jump on the majoritarian bandwagon. They see Cooper's Jason Newcome, who rejects all societal conventions because his community has not adequately justified its code to him, preferring to force it on him at an early age. In short, they see an imperfect system—but err in arguing that its shortcomings result from the inadequacy of its promise, rather than from the entanglements of hierarchy, the stifling brand of egalitarianism,[19] and improper forms of education.

The stories of Huck Finn and Silas Lapham illustrate the difficulty in carving out a space for the individual within society. As long as they remain in their settled lives, Huck and Silas are unable to evaluate their community's norms objectively. It is only when they begin their odysseys (via the Mississippi River or financial ruin) that they begin to perceive the world with fresh eyes. They see the insufficiency of their respective social codes, and allow other impulses (friendship, concern for others, appreciation of higher values) to rise to the surface.

American writers tend to be suspicious of society, fearing its tendency to stifle individuality. Huck Finn's last words are indicative of this feeling: "I reckon I got to light out for the Territory ahead of the rest, because Aunt Sally she's going to adopt me and sivilize me and I can't stand it. I been there before" (*HF* 366).[20] Yet Cooper, Twain, and Howells are not opposed to so-

---

19. That is, equality conceived of as similarity, rather than equally dignified individuality.

20. As Michael Wilding points out, Twain's misspelling of *civilize* "indicates the ironical

ciety per se; they simply seek a form of community in which norms are grounded in individual consent and are open to critical evaluation.[21] In this respect, the novelists are solid liberals, recognizing the importance of social ties, but ensuring that those ties are subject to revision and rejection. Though constitutional democracy, as found in the United States, emphasizes the importance of such deliberation in public debate, the novelists wish to extend this spirit beyond the political realm to all social relations. It is only in such a system that the individual can become more than a potentiality, and democratic liberty can be fully justified.

---

judgment that the sivilization Huck observes isn't really civilization." Wilding, *Political Fictions,* 21.

21. For the prevalence of such a view in the nineteenth century, see Howe, *Making the American Self,* 109; and Zuckert, *American Imagination,* chap. 1. Myra Jehlen has made the intriguing argument that the self-reliant individuals of nineteenth-century American literature all failed to create private, nonsocial worlds, and that every escape from society led either to death or to a return to society. Jehlen, "The Novel and the Middle Class," in Sacvan Bercovitch and Myra Jehlen, eds., *Ideology and Classic American Literature,* 125–44.

3

The Democratic Struggle
and Individual Development

SO FAR, WE HAVE SEEN HOW certain nineteenth- and twentieth-century critics characterized liberal democracy as incapable of elevating citizens' cultural level. Without the presence of some force, such as an aristocracy or a powerful state, to prompt individual development, they argued, democracy will inevitably end in mediocrity, for when people are allowed to rule themselves, unguided by social superiors, they tend to pursue more immediate, material ends. A society full of such people can perhaps hope for peace and prosperity, but will fail to reach its potential as a community of fully developed, fully *human* beings. In the preceding chapter, though, I discussed the ways in which Cooper, Twain, and Howells illustrate how the effects of incomplete liberation are often mistaken for those of liberation, and how the unsophisticated behavior that critics observe in democrats often results not from freedom and equality, but from the habits that remain after the hierarchical institutions that gave rise to them have disappeared. We also examined how the novelists' works demonstrate that liberation from hierarchy removes the scales from people's eyes and enables them to see the world for themselves—a necessary precondition for the development of their faculties.

However, we are still left with the problem of fully liberated democrats—people who are free from outside control and can see the world for themselves—failing to develop abilities not related to the pursuit of wealth. As T. S. Eliot notes, a liberal society does not give preference to nobler ideals in the marketplace of ideas. He and the other critics argue that under conditions of free choice, the average person will be more likely to appreciate material comfort than wisdom (unless wisdom is seen as a means to comfort). Liberation may make the pursuit of base ends more genuine, in that individuals will be choosing them for themselves, but it cannot make people realize that the ends they choose are in fact *base*. What is needed, then, is an argument for how liberation itself can provide an elevating force in the lives of democrats.

In this chapter, I shall outline how democratic liberty performs such a function, drawing again upon the works of Cooper, Twain, and Howells. In a nutshell, by placing citizens in a position where they must continually strive for autonomy, democracy serves to develop their faculties to a greater degree than aristocracy does. This may seem counterintuitive at first, since leisure from ordinary work (an aristocratic privilege) is often considered vital for the improvement of one's abilities. However, democrats possess certain advantages that compensate for their relative lack of leisure.

Like the aristocrat, the democrat is a ruler of both herself and her community. She looks upon nature as something to master and conform to her will. She is no one's inferior, and is responsible for her own actions; it is up to her how she develops her abilities. At this point, however, the democrat and aristocrat diverge. The aristocrat lives off the labor of his social inferiors, who provide for his basic wants. Except in extraordinary circumstances, he need not worry about where his next meal is coming from. As far as survival is concerned, his fellow aristocrats, not material necessity, are the chief threat to his safety. In contrast, the democrat is never secure in her mastery. She has no political superior, but she also has no inferiors to provide for her. Physical survival is an ever-present concern, and she has little time in her busy day for quiet reflection. Her self-mastery is difficult to maintain in the face of nature's challenges, and always a bit tenuous. However, it is these very challenges that prompt the development of her abilities. In her daily struggle with nature, she becomes sharper, more self-sufficient, better attuned to the workings of her environment, and more confident in thought and action. Since no one cushions her life by giving her commands or providing for her daily wants, she must take responsibility for a greater range of activities than her aristocratic counterpart.

Just as a medieval baron needed to be competent in the art of warfare to survive feudal squabbles, the democrat must develop the particular abilities needed to survive in her own harsh world. Whereas the baron chiefly struggled against other people, the democrat struggles in addition against the impersonal forces of nature. Liberal institutions may protect her from the aggressions of her neighbors, but they do not shield her from the broader demands of her environment. To maintain a level of autonomy, the democrat must labor in a variety of ways: as wage earner, household manager, parent, and so forth; failing in any of these capacities significantly decreases her control over her destiny.

The necessity of possessing a certain ability tends to call forth the development of that ability. The democrat, for whom survival is a daily challenge, is constantly forced to reassert mastery over her environment. In doing so, she engages her surroundings more fully than the leisured aristocrat, who in his leisure can be remarkably isolated from what occurs around him. One's level of individual development, rather than being in direct proportion to the amount of leisure time one enjoys, is more often in inverse proportion: the more one *struggles* to achieve mastery over one's surroundings, the greater are the forces triggering the cultivation of certain faculties, and thus greater the level of individual development. Leisure time is of course vital to individual development, by providing rest and time to reflect, but without an active, engaged life to prompt and guide reflection, leisure simply becomes an opportunity for laziness.

The fact that freedom itself can trigger individual development is good news for defenders of liberal democracy. As a result of the twentieth century's twin horrors of Nazism and Fascism, liberals are warier than ever about entrusting culture to the care of any institution, even a state controlled by the people. In the interest of preserving rights and liberties, they largely set aside the issue of cultural development, correctly believing it to be less important than preserving people from harm—in particular those forms of cruelty inflicted in the name of preserving a national culture.[1]

---

1. As Judith Shklar notes, the "liberalism of fear," by putting cruelty "unconditionally first, with nothing above us to excuse or to forgive acts of cruelty . . . closes off any appeal to any order other than that of actuality." Liberal democracy of this form, rather than being a "project for the perfectibility of mankind," is more a "recipe for survival." Shklar, *Ordinary Vices*, 4, 9.

However, if it can be shown that cultural development can be triggered in the absence of positive state action, it will be possible at the same time to preserve extensive rights and liberties.

In his critique of Mill, James Fitzjames Stephen argues that removing restraints generally does little to develop people's capacities. "Habitual exertion," he argues, "is the greatest of all invigorators of character, and restraint and coercion in one form or another is the great stimulus to exertion."[2] Mill's theory of liberty, Stephen points out, destroys traditional sources of cultural elevation without providing any replacements—other than a faith that genius will sprout forth when restraints are removed. On this point Stephen is largely correct, though we need not endorse using state power to coerce individual development. What both Mill and Stephen overlook is how conditions of equal liberty not only serve as a precondition for individual development, but in fact supply a form of elevating coercion of their own.

Yet the outlook is not quite rosy. As the novelists illustrate, the democratic struggle tends to produce individuals who, though sharp and well developed in certain respects, are nevertheless narrow in outlook. In their fight for mastery over their environment, they acquire only those skills that are directly related to the task at hand. Democrats may be more broadly developed than warring medieval barons, but this is not enough to gain the respect of the aesthetic critics, who are unimpressed by the achievement of physical comfort, however grand. The struggle for mastery can indeed serve as the basis for full development, but it cannot provide all the resources necessary for achieving it. Only when the struggle of free people is combined with a functioning democratic public sphere (see Chapter 4) can fuller development occur and the aesthetic critique be refuted.

The Aristocratic Experience

Aristocracy, the rule by the best, depends for its survival on a clear distinction between noble and common—that is, between those traits exhibited by all people and those that reflect an excellent character. Shunning passivity and conformity, aristocrats chiefly value individual courage and

2. Stephen, *Liberty, Equality, Fraternity,* 31.

honor. They avoid labor, considering it stunting and degrading. Just as pulling a plow may be perfectly acceptable for a plodding Percheron, but will ruin a thoroughbred's spirit, the aristocrat's excellence depends on a certain freedom from the cares of daily existence. As Aristotle pointed out, in the best state "the citizens must not lead the life of artisans or tradesmen, for such a life is ignoble and inimical to excellence. Neither must they be farmers, since leisure is necessary both for the development of excellence and the performance of political duties."[3]

Underlying this assertion is the belief that individual development can only occur when people have time to relax and reflect. On this argument, mindless labor stifles independent thought and distracts people from pursuing a political or contemplative life. By delegating menial tasks to subordinates, aristocrats can devote greater time to study and self-improvement. Of course, the activities aristocrats pursue in their leisure time vary considerably, from the tournaments of the Middle Ages to the elegant dinner parties of nineteenth-century sophisticates. However, all these practices are linked by a common end: the development of faculties that will distinguish aristocrats as excellent human beings, superior to everyday man.

One can easily appreciate the argument that leisure is essential to the full flowering of human abilities. If a person works all day, how will he find sufficient time for cultivating faculties unrelated to his job? To the average person, leisure is a privilege, something enjoyed by aristocrats and the wealthy. However, as Twain and Howells demonstrate, leisure and privilege—of whatever form—are insufficient for individual development. When not embedded in a life of physical and mental activity, they argue, leisure serves no purpose. Instead, it tends to make people complacent and satisfied with the status quo. Sensing this, Aristotle advises legislators to "secure leisure" for the best citizens while they are in office, but is careful not to equate this leisure with freedom from all responsibilities; as the "first principle of all action," leisure involves preparation as well as relaxation.[4]

The problem with leisure chiefly arises when it becomes disjoined from activity. The best citizens in a newly founded aristocracy may indeed be able to use leisure productively, since they initially proved their worth through

---

3. Aristotle, *The Politics*, bk. 7, chap. 9, 1328b39–1329a2.
4. Ibid., bk. 2, chap. 11, 1273b5–8; bk. 8, chap. 3, 1337b33.

virtuous action, but it is less certain that their successors will do the same. As Thomas Paine points out, "virtue is not hereditary."[5] Too often the world has seen keen, heroic aristocracies soften and bloat over the course of generations—the result of giving special privileges to people based on their ancestry, not their virtue. Most typical is the type of aristocracy that remains excellent in one or more areas (for example, warfare or the arts), but fails to demonstrate excellence in other important areas. Twain's depiction of Camelot, with its chivalrous warrior knights, and Howells's description of the easygoing sophisticate Bromfield Corey both illustrate this tendency toward partial development under conditions of aristocratic leisure.

Hank Morgan's opinion of King Arthur's realm must be taken with a grain of salt, given his decidedly Yankee point of view, but his general description of Camelot is quite revealing. The Knights of the Round Table are highly skilled warriors, capable of defending the kingdom against damsel-snatching ogres, infidels, and the like. They operate according to a strict code of conduct, and practice their craft in elaborate jousting tournaments. As Hank notes, "There was a fine manliness observable in almost every face; and in some a certain loftiness and sweetness" (*CY* 14). Camelot values battle prowess above all, and meetings at the Round Table consist of highly exaggerated retellings of past escapades.

Although Hank is skeptical about the legitimacy of a political system that privileges a small minority of the population at the expense of the remainder, it is hardly surprising how such a hierarchy evolved. Given the danger of military conquest by neighboring kingdoms and the advantages (in pre-firearm days) of fighting on horseback, those men who could prove their skill with lance and sword were more deserving of power than the common foot soldier. The perception of danger served to drive the development of military excellence (notwithstanding the fact that many of the threats facing Camelot—such as ogres—were imagined), and the nature of the survival struggle (competition between petty rulers) governed the form of the development.

Despite the high level of military skill and bravery the Arthurian nobles exhibit, Hank finds that they remain stunted in other key respects: "There did not seem to be brains enough in the entire nursery, so to speak, to bait

5. Thomas Paine, *Common Sense*, 110.

a fishhook with; but you didn't seem to mind that, after a little, because you soon saw that brains were not needed in a society like that, and, indeed would have marred it, hindered it, spoiled its symmetry—perhaps rendered its existence impossible" (*CY* 14). In a society where there is no force prodding people to develop in certain directions, leisure will not supply the deficiency. Medieval society rewarded skills related to mounted warfare, not intelligence or sophistication. Superstitions abound in Camelot, and with a few clever pranks Hank is able to convince even Arthur of his "magical" powers. Accompanying superstition is widespread subservience to the Church, whose interdict rolls back Hank's civilizing plan and unites the country's nobles against him. Before the interdict, Hank had been able to control the Church, like Arthur, through various gimmicks and tricks, but in the end the power of organized religion was irresistible. Because for so long the Church had thought for people, it was nearly impossible for them to break free and think for themselves. Even Hank's man factories are only partially successful in training people to be humans, as most of Camelot's residents desire security (even if in the form of Church authority) more than their own humanity.

The same stunted behavior can be seen in other areas of Arthurian life. Besides the code of chivalry, which came into being primarily to regulate aristocratic warfare, knights and ladies act according to few rules of conduct. As Hank notes, the glorious Camelot of yore is in reality as tidy as a common pigsty, and "many of the terms used in the most matter-of-fact way by this great assemblage of the first ladies and gentlemen in the land would have made a Comanche blush" (*CY* 20). No one realizes the indelicacy of their everyday customs, which are no better than those of the commoners. The Arthurian aristocrats are simply ordinary medieval people placed in ruling positions based on a small set of abilities they happen to possess. When given the privileges of aristocrats, they hone their military talents, but the added leisure does little for the rest of their abilities. They remain as common as before—and possibly worse, given the ill effects of leisure when detached from excellent activity.

What Twain's depiction of Camelot demonstrates is that giving aristocratic privileges to the best members of the community, in addition to violating democratic conceptions of justice, often does little to maintain and improve the excellence of those members. Only when the luxuries of being a master, including leisure, are linked to an active, productive life in the world will those luxuries prompt individual development. Paradoxically, only when the ruling class is uncertain of its position in the social hierarchy does it tend to exhibit its most valuable qualities. Only when aristocrats are insecure in their leisure, when their privileges are threatened, and when they must struggle to maintain their position, do they tend to develop their abilities and become worthy of ruling.

However, this is not an experience we typically associate with aristocracies. Aristocrats, who pride themselves on being immune from degrading forms of labor, usually fear their peers more than nature. Challenges to their authority (foreign aggression, peasant revolts) do not threaten their status as aristocrats, since such challenges may be met with military force (defined broadly). Regardless of the outcome, the aristocrat remains free from material necessity. If he loses, he can rest assured he did not degrade himself; he retains his aristocratic mind-set even if removed from his privileged place in the hierarchy. However, if other cares and concerns, especially material necessity, threaten his position, and he finds he must labor to provide for his daily needs, he may remain an aristocrat in name, but has ceased to be one in spirit. He has become more like a democrat, who cannot depend on the labor of others for his sustenance.

Howells's Bromfield Corey is acutely aware of this fact, and his reluctance to let Tom join Silas Lapham's mineral-paint business stems from his aristocratic principles. Bromfield, who inherited a modest fortune from his merchantman father, takes pride in the fact that he need not work to support his life of leisure. He considers self-made men like Silas vulgar, and decries their attempts to buy their way into high society. Rather than surrender his patrician attitudes toward wealth gathering, he maintains his life of aristocratic leisure by scrimping and saving, all the while hoping that Tom will marry into a wealthy Brahmin family. Only partly in jest, he chides his son for his worldly ambition, pointing out that "we shall never have a real aristocracy while this plebeian reluctance to live upon a parent or a wife continues the animating spirit of our youth. It strikes at the root of the whole feudal system" (*SL* 64–65, 67).

However, despite his elegant manners and refined sensibilities, Bromfield remains only partially developed. Silas, though himself a man of limited outlook, is quick to recognize Bromfield's shortcomings. To him, Bromfield exhibits all the bad tendencies of aristocrats: he never does a stitch of work, he speaks condescendingly of those with fewer privileges, and he spends all his time reading French magazines and contemplating art. As a young man, Bromfield had refused to enter his father's business, choosing instead to travel to Europe and study art in Rome. Though somewhat talented as an artist, Bromfield was never inspired to develop his abilities in that direction. After ten years of living off his father's fortune, he came home and married into wealth. Financially set for life, he "continued a dilettante, never quite abandoning his art, but working at it fitfully, and talking more about it than working at it." Fearing that Tom Corey will follow his father's example, Silas brings him into his own business; after all, he notes, "I like to see a man *act* like a man. I don't like to see him taken care of like a young lady" (*SL* 58, 70).

Bromfield had limitless opportunities as a privileged young man, but none of the ambition that comes from an engaged life. His son, perhaps realizing the insufficiency of that lifestyle for achieving a satisfying life, sets out to make his own fortune. In doing so, he complements his refined sensibilities with a healthy ambition, gained through struggle with the world (recall that Tom joined Silas's enterprise as it had begun to fall apart; his experience was thus far from the aristocratic ease of his father). By the end of the book, Tom serves as a sort of ideal man, a compromise between Bromfield Corey, the refined but loafing aristocrat, and Silas Lapham, the crude but engaged self-made man.

Twain and Howells demonstrate that leisure divorced from a life of struggle with one's environment does little for individual development. Unless some other force motivates development, leisure can at best only provide relaxation. By insulating people from the invigorating experience of making one's own way in the world, it may even cause their senses to be dulled, preventing the cultivation of their abilities. At any rate, Twain and Howells effectively refute the critics' assertion that giving disproportionate political power to certain classes of excellent people will necessarily elevate society as a whole.

The Democratic Experience

Modern democracy grants equal liberty to all, regardless of birth, wealth, or excellence. Unlike aristocratic regimes, democracy recognizes no formal political distinction between noble and common. Though there is substantial room within egalitarian societies for people to distinguish themselves, such inequality is considered legally and politically irrelevant. Because of this equal liberty, the democrat lives in a peculiar state of isolation. Since she is no longer part of an elaborate hierarchy, no one can order her to do anything against her will (though she may grant authority through her consent, as in a social covenant). She is judged not on the basis of her social rank, but by the nature of her actions. She can think for herself and see the world with her own eyes. She can become whatever she wishes, and can renounce communal obligations if necessary. Though most democrats choose to remain linked to communities (family, city, nation), they nonetheless possess the ability to reject their inherited social roles, unlike serfs and peasants.

With freedom, however, comes responsibility. Just as no one issues directives from above, under democracy no one supplies daily wants from below. In hierarchical societies, noblesse oblige and the necessity of maintaining one's property prompt superiors to care for their inferiors, but under democracy each citizen must struggle to make her own living. A democratic citizen can neither rely on the protection and provision of a superior, nor live off the labor of inferiors. She is a ruler, but not like an aristocrat. She must constantly strive to exercise control over her environment and maintain her democratic independence. She is threatened not only by her rivals (the chief danger in aristocratic societies) but by nature itself, which places demands on her at all times and in a variety of ways.

Knowing that poverty or death is the reward for laziness, the democrat supports herself through work. Yet democratic work, though its primary end is subsistence, is not the same as that of a serf. While the serf labors for the sake of someone else, the democrat works for herself. The serf's master provides him with the bare necessities of life (and no more or less), but the democrat's comfort depends on the amount of work she performs. (I assume typical liberal legal provisions are in place to prevent people from harming each other and stealing the fruits of each other's labor; otherwise, there would be a large disjunction between work and comfort.) She finds that greater effort generally produces greater comfort, and consequently devotes her energies to increasing her output. As Cooper and Howells demonstrate, this struggle for survival and prosperity in the face of material necessity sharpens and develops the democratic individual more fully than her aristocratic counterpart, whether in the context of the frontier or modern industrial society.

I use the terms *work* and *labor* interchangeably, since in common usage the distinction between them is not nearly as pronounced as, for example, in Hannah Arendt's work. For my purposes, it is enough that both concepts denote the expending of energy in purposive activity. Nor do I rely heavily upon Abraham Lincoln's discussion of free labor in his "Address to the Wisconsin State Agricultural Society." In a society where nearly everyone works for someone else, and where working for wages carries little stigma, it is unreasonable to adhere strictly to Lincoln's yeoman ideal. However, one could argue that modern wage earners achieve a degree of autonomy similar to that of independent farmers, thus satisfying Lincoln's conditions for free labor.[6]

At the beginning of *The Pioneers,* Cooper describes how wealthy Europeans initially had difficulty settling in the wilds of colonial America: "Accustomed to ease, and unequal to the struggles incident to an infant society, the affluent emigrant was barely enabled to maintain his own rank by the weight of his personal superiority and acquirements; but, the moment that his head was laid in the grave, his indolent and comparatively uneducated offspring were compelled to yield precedency to the more active energies of a class whose exertions had been stimulated by necessity" (*P* 557). Those who had enjoyed aristocratic privileges in the Old World were now being tested in a much harsher environment. Without an institutionalized hierarchy, and with a social elite incapable of handling the pressures of the New World, the American colonies were ripe for a social revolution, and Cooper deftly illustrates how the democratic conditions of the frontier elevated the common man by putting his abilities sharply to the test.

Natty Bumppo appears for the first time in *The Pioneers,* depicted as an aging man of the woods unable to adapt to settlement life. Natty is perhaps the supreme example of how liberation itself calls forth excellence, having learned on his own how to live in the wilderness, survive on his hunting skills, and avoid the dangers of the forest. His relation to his environment is unmediated, and he can intuit the order in his surroundings. However,

6. Hannah Arendt, *The Human Condition;* Abraham Lincoln, "Address to the Wisconsin State Agricultural Society, Milwaukee, Wisconsin," in *Selected Speeches and Writings.*

this direct relationship would be insufficient for the development of Natty's abilities without a corresponding instinct for survival. This desire, because so fundamental and natural, ensures that when placed in a harsh world without the protection of a benevolent hierarchy, Natty will actively work to survive—not throw up his hands in despair.

Cooper has often been dismissed as overly romantic, based on Natty's superhuman feats of marksmanship and woodcraft.[7] However, given Cooper's intention such a charge is largely unfounded. He is careful throughout the Leatherstocking Tales not to attribute Natty's skills to advantages of birth (Natty is far from handsome and has received little formal education), thus isolating the effects of experience on his development. Hurry Harry, for example, possesses many of the natural advantages Natty lacks, yet falls short of his achievements, due to his different life experiences (*DS* 7–8, 171). The question of plausibility, then, turns on whether Cooper convincingly describes the relationship between people's abilities and the environment in which they live.

Cooper's portrayal of Natty may still be open to the charge of romanticism, but his embellishments advance the purpose of his tales. Just as Natty serves as a model for ordinary people as they free themselves from past prejudices and hierarchies (see Chapter 2), he also demonstrates how conditions of democratic liberty promote individual development. Although most people do not (and cannot) live lives as free as Natty's, they can look to him to see the effects of extensive liberty on the development of human faculties, and shape their own lives accordingly.

Billy Kirby is a relatively minor character in *The Pioneers,* but he represents Cooper's concern with the individual development of all democratic citizens.[8] Kirby, an accomplished Vermont woodsman, becomes one of the

---

7. The most famous critique is Mark Twain, "Fenimore Cooper's Literary Offenses," in *The Portable Mark Twain,* 541–46. Howard Mumford Jones derides Twain's approach, however, comparing his essay to "an account of Shakespeare's technique that confined itself to putting Bohemia on the seacoast, letting Cleopatra play billiards in Alexandria, and having a clock strike three in Caesar's Rome." Jones, *Jeffersonianism and the American Novel,* 28. On this point, see also Sydney J. Krause, *Mark Twain as Critic,* 128–47.

8. Arthur Mizener contends that "Cooper makes even his minor characters into lucid embodiments of powerful and typical moral attitudes and uses the exciting action of his story to dramatize the conflicts among these attitudes." Mizener, *Twelve Great American Novels,* 8. Though Mizener is referring in this passage to Hurry Harry and Tom Hutter, the same is true of Billy Kirby.

earliest settlers of Templeton (a literary version of Cooperstown, New York). Cooper notes that Kirby, "whose occupation, when he did labor, was that of clearing lands, or chopping jobs, was of great stature, and carried, in his very air, the index of his character. He was a noisy, boisterous, reckless lad, whose good-natured eye contradicted the bluntness and bullying tenor of his speech." Preferring idleness to the loss of independence that permanent employment would entail, Kirby would lounge in the taverns between the odd jobs that sustained him. However, when a prospective employer would offer him wages commensurate to his abilities, he would "shoulder his ax and his rifle, slip his arms through the straps of his pack, and enter the woods with the tread of a Hercules." Once at work, knowing that his livelihood and reputation depended on his labors, he would put his heart into it:

> For days, weeks, nay months, Bill Kirby would toil with an ardor that evinced his native spirit, and with an effect that seemed magical, until, his chopping being ended, his stentorian lungs could be heard emitting sounds, as he called to his patient oxen, which rang through the hills like the cries of an alarm. . . . His piles, or to use the language of the country, his logging, ended, with a dispatch that could only accompany his dexterity and herculean strength, the jobber would collect together his implements of labor, light the heaps of timber, and march away under the blaze of the prostrate forest, like the conqueror of some city, who, having first prevailed over his adversary, applies the torch as the finishing blow to his conquest.

Because Kirby must rely upon himself to earn his bread, he has a powerful motivation for improving his abilities. To be sure, he tends to be lazy at times, but that is not a direct result of democratic liberty. Rather, it reflects his knack for earning enough money to maintain himself during slack periods. He has become such a master of his surroundings that he can afford to take a break (P 643).

Cooper's descriptions of Kirby are full of phrases suggesting conquest and domination (such as the analogy to the city conqueror in the passage above). Through long practice Kirby has become an excellent lumberjack, capable of clearing vast areas of timber with great efficiency. He knows the exact type of effort required to fell a given tree, and his actions are expert and refined, like the "salutes of a fencing master." From the moment of his first measuring blow, "the sounds of the ax were ceaseless, while the falling of the trees was like a distant cannonading; and the daylight broke into the depths of the woods with the suddenness of a winter morning." Kirby's mastery over his surroundings is also evident in his marksmanship (second only to Natty's) and his flair for making maple sugar. He knows how the world works, and can get the best out of it for himself. Nor is he completely innocent of how society works. Though ostensibly a rough man of the settlements, he does not fall for the subtle jests of the aristocratic Mr. Le Quoi; sensing the latter has been making fun of his sugaring business, he meekly gives him a boiling-hot cup of syrup to drink—correctly guessing the Frenchman would underestimate his ability to respond to sophisticated humor. The syrup scalds Le Quoi's throat, bringing forth "such swearing and spitting in French you never saw." Kirby remarks that "it's a knowing one, from the old countries, that thinks to get his jokes smoothly over a woodchopper" (*P* 643, 663).

Despite his rough edges, Kirby is fairly well developed and worthy of respect. He has successfully mastered his environment, making it yield in abundance the necessities of life, and is servant to no man. His constant struggle to maintain his democratic independence has sharpened his mind and strengthened his spirit, making him the equal of any person, noble or common. Because democratic life is challenging in a greater variety of ways than aristocratic life is—chiefly because self-rule in a democracy is more tenuous—the effect on individual development is richer and broader. Unlike Arthur's knights, who developed skills in a limited number of areas (chiefly centered around making war), Kirby becomes a multifaceted, reasonably well-rounded individual.[9]

What would become of Billy Kirby if he were to enjoy the privileges of an aristocrat? Would he still acquire the unaffected virtues of democratic life? Or, knowing his material wants would be satisfied, would he instead sink into a life of idleness? Since Cooper tells us that Kirby usually needed some prodding before agreeing to go to work, the likelihood is small that

9. John Cawelti asserts that Cooper rejects the ideal of the self-made man. Cawelti, *Apostles of the Self-Made Man*, 78–80. To some degree Cooper's *American Democrat*, when considered in isolation, lends itself to that interpretation. However, Cooper's novels—especially *The Pioneers*—offer a more complex account of self-making, and *The American Democrat* should be read in this context.

he would cultivate his abilities without such encouragement. The aesthetic critics argue that some form of aristocratic hierarchy is necessary to elevate a nation's cultural level, but they make two fundamental errors. First, they overlook the fact that a life of privilege, divorced from active engagement with the world, is not particularly conducive to the development of the higher faculties. Since leisure does not call forth virtue by itself, it is unwise to entrust the task of cultural elevation to a privileged, leisure-enjoying class. Carlyle, Yeats, Pound, and Eliot are certainly vulnerable to this counterargument, as are Mill and Arnold to a lesser degree. Second, the critics disregard how democratic liberation provides its own elevating force, even in the lives of ordinary people. Those critics who sidestepped the first argument are vulnerable to this one. All the critics agree that only some people can use liberty wisely, and that everyone else would do well to defer to that elite. Yet as the novelists have shown, this is a superficial—and consequently skewed—view of democracy's tendencies. Only by recognizing both these facts can we explain why Kirby, who prefers idleness to work, comes to develop his abilities.

Intent upon defending American democracy from its critics, Cooper finds much to admire in the sturdy settlers of the frontier, the future bedrock of the republic. Billy Kirby, like millions of subsequent Americans, flourishes under conditions of equal liberty because democracy grants him authority over his own life, but makes the exercise of that authority difficult. Kirby is responsible for his own well-being, and struggles to assert dominance over his environment for his *own* comfort, not that of some master. Leisure, rather than being a precondition for his development, is his reward—which he certainly deserves, having proven his abilities.

Howells draws an even clearer connection between liberty and individual development. In *A Hazard of New Fortunes,* a social novel of late nineteenth-century Manhattan, Howells tells of the rise of another self-made man, Jacob Dryfoos, who discovers that his Indiana farm lies over a reservoir of natural gas. After selling his land for a considerable sum, he moves his family to New York, where he increases his fortune through stock speculation. Though rapid success hardens his heart and in some respects dulls his faculties (an issue I will address shortly), Dryfoos nonetheless becomes a greater man under democratic conditions than if he had enjoyed aristocratic ease from childhood.

Before his meteoric rise to fortune, Dryfoos had been a respectable farmer and one of the leading citizens of his community. He possessed solid horse sense, and through hard work and careful management made a modest income from the land. The fact that he achieved his prosperity through old-fashioned virtue caused his community to elect him justice of the peace, school trustee, and county commissioner. As a local leader, he opposed any measures, such as the sale of a public canal to the railroads, that would place his town under the control of big business, no matter how benevolent. Because of his "intense individualism," Dryfoos "suspected all expense of being spendthrift," and was wary of any outside authority telling him how to live his life. After the discovery of natural gas, he tried his best to convince his neighbors not to sell their farms to Standard Oil. In his opinion, "it wouldn't be five years before the Standard owned the whole region"—thereby making impossible the modest virtues brought forth under conditions of democratic liberty. However, the trust's giant bankroll quickly overwhelmed the farmers' willpower, and even Dryfoos was persuaded to sell out. Like most of his neighbors, he bought a house in town, knowing the interest from his new riches would support his family indefinitely (*HNF* 75–77, 225–26).

He soon realizes that his fortune, by removing all fear of material necessity, is softening his character. He complains to his friends: "I hain't got any horses, I hain't got any cows, I hain't got any pigs, I hain't got any chickens. I hain't got anything to do from sunup to sundown." Without any challenges to his abilities, he knows he is on a developmental plateau; his life of ease, though pleasant, frustrates his desire to become a fuller human being. Seeking a testing field for his abilities, he becomes a real estate speculator. The experience of again earning money and actively mastering his environment—as he does even more successfully when he begins investing in railroads and mines—is therapeutic for Dryfoos. His greater experience of the world and its workings enhances his native common sense. Not only is he able to amass a sizable amount of wealth and move to New York, but he also becomes a more highly developed individual as a result of his new democratic struggle (*HNF* 77).

Fulkerson, the promoter of the literary journal in which Dryfoos invests, notes that although Dryfoos has become inflexible in some respects, "he ha[s] expanded in others to the full measure of the vast scale on which he did business." Faced with the uncertainties of democratic life, Dryfoos has developed "a courage, a magnanimity, that [is] equal to the strain." Attributing his development to "the versatility of the American mind and . . . the grandeur of institutions and opportunities that let every man grow to his full size," Fulkerson notes that "old Dryfoos could step into Bismarck's shoes and run the German Empire at ten days' notice or about as long as it would take him to go from New York to Berlin." To him, Dryfoos embodies what is at least part of the American Dream: compelled to take care of himself, he uses his resources and environment to best advantage, thereby achieving a position of relative mastery and independence. To be sure, he begins his rise to riches with Standard Oil money already in his pocket, but this alone does not distinguish him from Billy Kirby or other self-made individuals. It is the struggle for autonomy in the face of a harsh environment that tends to bring out the best in people; where they begin (financially or otherwise) is somewhat less important (*HNF* 184–85).

The novelists remind us of the complexity of the democratic experience. For them, unlike the critics, democratic liberation involves much more than the mere lifting of restraints. By giving all people—whether noble or common—power over their own lives and responsibility for their actions, equal liberty dramatically restructures the relationship between them and their surroundings. Their everyday struggle for independence from material want and outside control calls forth a variety of abilities—abilities that otherwise would have remained dormant. Though under hierarchical conditions Billy Kirby and Jacob Dryfoos might have made decent peasants or aristocrats, they reach their fullest level of development under democracy, a regime that makes all people masters without servants. The democrat is alone in the world, a fact that causes her to become *capable* of being alone in the world.

Arrogant Materialism

Although democratic liberty is, on the whole, conducive to individual development, certain of its effects are less than desirable. Like the critics, the novelists are quick to point out these pitfalls of equal liberty, three of which I shall discuss here. The first involves the complacence that success breeds, and the second relates to inequality under liberalism, while the third concerns the narrowness of individual development under democracy.

First, if the democratic struggle for autonomy calls forth abilities that enhance people's mastery over their surroundings, what happens when an adequate level of mastery has been achieved? If, like Dryfoos, a person becomes successful and enjoys the same freedom from material necessity as aristocrats do, what becomes of the driving force behind development? Would we not expect the fortunate person to slacken his efforts and sink into idleness? Does individual development, the further it proceeds, destroy the initial cause for development?

This question can be answered in part by noting that there is no real end to bourgeois striving. What the democrat seeks, he cannot have: the safe, privileged lifestyle of the aristocrat. No matter what he does, he will never be more than his neighbor's political equal. However, wealth offers privileges similar to those of aristocracy, which prompts people at all socioeconomic levels constantly to seek greater material fortune—and consequently, to continue to develop their abilities. Democratic "success" has an ambiguous nature. For example, how do we know when someone has become successful? When he exceeds the poverty line? When he has enough money to send his children to private universities? When he has three cars, a summer home, and a yacht? At what point has he achieved an adequate level of mastery over his environment? The fact that this is a difficult question to answer suggests that the struggle for mastery under democratic conditions can continue indefinitely—regardless of what level of income one has achieved. Bourgeois democrats continually strive for more complete control over their destiny, not realizing that what they desire is impossible to attain under an egalitarian regime. They must live with the fact that no matter how much money they make, they will never enjoy the safe, privileged lifestyle of aristocrats. Regardless of their affluence, they will always be their neighbors' political equal, and nothing more. However, since the privileges of wealth are similar to those of aristocracy, people at all levels seek to move up the socioeconomic ladder, continually developing their abilities as they climb.

While it is true that aristocrats also wish to increase their wealth and dominion, the process by which they achieve these goals is different. If King Arthur wants to improve his standing vis-à-vis his rivals, he strives for political or military victory over them. Once he has conquered their territories, he has achieved his goal; the subsequent task of maintaining the peace does little to challenge and develop his abilities. If he wishes to live in greater material luxury, he simply issues a command to his inferiors, and they will provide for his every want. This sort of material improvement, though it may continue as indefinitely as material advancement under democracy, does not develop the aristocrat's character, beyond giving him experience in managing tool-like humans. The aristocrat, even as he rises in condition, encounters his environment solely as a secure master; he does not experience the uneasiness that characterizes democratic life—and gives the democrat richer insight into his surroundings.

The second problem is more serious. As some people become successful, those at the bottom may find it increasingly difficult to improve their position. Because poverty prevents them from achieving even a modest level of autonomy, their labor resembles that of slaves: they are always working for someone higher up, and only experience life from the perspective of the social subordinate. To be sure, their daily struggle tests their abilities, but they are never able to view life as an autonomous being. Just as the aristocrat sees the world solely from on high, the poor man sees it only from the bottom. Neither perspective by itself is conducive to development; only when combined, as in the democrat's *uncertain* mastery, can they call forth the full range of human abilities.

Republican theorists have often noted the importance of rough material equality for cultivating civic virtue within democratic polities,[10] but have largely overlooked the importance of limiting inequality for the sake of individual development as a whole. If, as Fulkerson states, the promise of America is to "let every man grow to his full size," we cannot help but be troubled when dire poverty permanently locks people into a subordinate social position. Howells in particular despises this aspect of American progress, juxtaposing Jacob Dryfoos's fabulous wealth against the congested, teeming slums of Manhattan's immigrant districts—as when Dryfoos's son is beaten to death during a streetcar-workers' strike. For Howells, the rigidity of castes does far more harm than good, degrading both the elite

---

10. See Sandel's *Democracy's Discontent* for a discussion of the civic argument against inequality. One classic statement of the republican case is found in Jean-Jacques Rousseau, *The Social Contract:* "If you wish to give the state cohesion, bring the limits of wealth and poverty as close together as possible: do not allow either extreme opulence or destitution. The two are inseparable by nature, and both are equally damaging to the common good; one produces the instruments of tyranny, and the other produces the tyrants" (87n).

(by enabling a life of idleness) and the masses (by binding them to a life of poverty).

The third weakness—and the one the aesthetic critics emphasize—is that the qualities democrats acquire through their struggle with nature, such as frugality, moderation, cleverness, and ingenuity, are all primarily oriented toward the goal of mastery over one's surroundings. As a result, the development of virtues is uneven, to the detriment of certain higher faculties. Beauty and wisdom are of no use to the striving democrat unless he can profit by them. He will continue to prefer knowledge that is more practical and will better help him achieve autonomy.

The novelists readily concede this point. Returning to Cooper's depiction of Billy Kirby, for example, we find that although Kirby is a fine worker with a good heart and a strong spirit, he is incredibly wasteful. Because he knows there will always be more trees to chop down, ensuring a continuous source of income, he strips the forests bare and burns the logs. His actions, though profitable both to himself and his employers, demonstrate a severe narrowness of outlook. He views the world simply as something to master and shape to his will, with little concern for its own welfare. In typical democratic fashion, he gives little thought to the finitude and harmony of his surroundings, unless such considerations serve his materialist purpose.

Kirby's ecological callousness extends beyond his slash-and-burn lumbering, for he exhibits a heartless attitude toward his environment even in the things he does for sport. For instance, he and his village friends go "fishing" one evening. Rather than tossing in a line and catching the fish they need, they set up a massive seine between two rowboats and drag hordes of helpless fish to shore in the net. Since the village can consume only a small portion of the catch, Kirby and his friends leave most of it to rot on the beach (calling to mind the carelessness of subsequent generations, such as the white buffalo hunters' custom of slaughtering their prey solely for their hides and tongues). Natty Bumppo observes the scene, and castigates the fishermen: "If they had fur, like the beaver, or you could tan their hides, like a buck, something might be said in favor of taking them by the thousand with your nets; but as God made them for man's food, and for no other disarnable reason, I call it sinful and wasty to catch more than can be eat." Squandering vast quantities of a precious resource becomes an egregious offense when done simply to affirm one's own sense of mastery over the world. Not satisfied even with catching enough for a village feast, Kirby plunders the lake to prove his domination over nature—just as when chopping timber, he selects the noblest tree in the forest as the "first trial of his power" (*P* 643, 683).

Because the democrat must conquer nature to achieve a degree of autonomy, he tends to take a more adversarial stance toward his surroundings than the aristocrat does. The struggle for autonomy is a contest of sorts, and it is not enough barely to scratch out a victory. That would imply that the victory is an insecure one, and that nature might win the next round. The democrat attempts to assuage this uncertainty through bravado, boasting of his exploits and lording it over his surroundings like "the conqueror of some city." Consequently, the democrat's initial developmental narrowness is sustained by his arrogance; and his benign neglect of higher faculties turns into a conscious repudiation of such values. Those virtues unrelated to controlling nature, such as a sense of ecology, are not only dismissed as impractical, but in fact even become signs of weakness. Those who exhibit concern for nature's balance, and who realize that their own autonomous actions can have detrimental effects on the world around them, are considered less worthy than those (like Kirby) who display the highest skill in bending objects to their will.[11]

As we have seen, Jacob Dryfoos is equally adept at manipulating his surroundings. However, he possesses a fault similar to Kirby's, in that as he develops as a democratic individual, he fails to cultivate the full range of his abilities. Only the virtues that serve his manipulations are desirable to him, which significantly constrains his outlook on life. As Basil March, the literary editor of Dryfoos's journal, remarks, Dryfoos's character had been fundamentally reshaped on the route to prosperity: "He must have undergone a moral deterioration, an atrophy of the generous instincts, and I don't see why it shouldn't have reached his mental makeup. He has sharpened, but he has narrowed; his sagacity has turned into suspicion, his caution to meanness, his courage to ferocity. That's the way I philosophize a man of

11. Donald A. Ringe hints at an interpretation similar to mine: "Only in *The Pioneers* does man meet nature on something like equal terms; but the illusion of dominance that some of the characters acquire leads to wanton, immoral waste of the resources they possess." Ringe, *James Fenimore Cooper*, 153.

Dryfoos' experience, and I am not very proud when I realize that such a man and his experience are the ideal and ambition of most Americans." To a refined man like March, Dryfoos represents the chief ills of the American social system. In his rise to fortune, Dryfoos has become even more selfish, materialistic, uncultured, and arrogant than before. He now despises and pities people who earn their money "painfully, slowly, and in little amounts," believing the quick gains of speculation worthy of greater honor. In coming to New York, Dryfoos looked forward to testing his wits against other self-made millionaires, who were "smart and got their money by sharp practices to which lesser men could not attain" (*HNF* 226–27).

Howells shows how Dryfoos's initial virtues, which like Kirby's had been brought forth through a struggle for autonomy, become increasingly sharper and narrower as his fortunes rise. By the time he comes to Manhattan, Dryfoos has become so skilled at bending the world to his will that his haughtiness blinds him to values other than wealth gathering. When his son, Conrad, wishes to become a minister, for example, Dryfoos assigns him a post at the journal—believing even the ministry to be a worthless profession, unless informed by a businessman's sense of the world. With the notable exception of Conrad, Dryfoos's family shares the arrogant materialism of their patriarch. Dryfoos's daughters, for example, cannot understand why their family's affluence does not gain them admittance to the highest circles of Manhattan society. As Howells explains,

> They had not learned enough at school to doubt [their equality with the wisest and the finest], and the splendor of their father's success in making money had blinded them forever to any possible difference against them. They had no question of themselves in the social abeyance to which they had been left in New York. They had been surprised, mystified; it was not what they had expected; there must be some mistake. They were the victims of an accident which would be repaired as soon as the fact of their father's wealth had got around. They had been steadfast in their faith, through all their disappointment, that they were not only better than most people by virtue of his money, but as good as any.

The Dryfooses fail to recognize any standard of value other than wealth, or any virtue not directly conducive to greater affluence. Because of their family's wealth-gathering excellence, they believe themselves socially superior to those who struggle and have less success. Their arrogance, of course, arises from ignorance of other elements of the good life, but it is arrogance nonetheless—and it sustains the Dryfooses' loyalty to the narrow bourgeois virtues. Consequently, it is even more difficult to reform the Dryfooses into broader, richer personalities, and by the end of *A Hazard of New Fortunes* this process has only just begun (triggered by Conrad's death) (*HNF* 224, 380–81).

Of the three problems discussed above (the tendency toward complacence caused by success, the stunting effects of vast inequality, and the narrowing effects of the democratic struggle), the third is closest to the heart of the aesthetic critique. If the struggle for mastery in fact narrows the democrat's soul, are not the critics vindicated? If Billy Kirby and Jacob Dryfoos develop only those capacities that bring them profit or a feeling of victory over their surroundings, what happens to the broader virtues that make up a well-rounded individual? If democrats cannot see beyond their own self-interest, preferring reckoning to reason, profit to philosophy, and conquest to culture, what are the consequences for the comparison between democracy and aristocracy? Seen in this light, aristocrats, though their leisure from work does little for their development, at least do not become, like Dryfoos, monstrous caricatures of practical virtue. Unless there is a way to take advantage of the democrat's unique developmental advantages while alleviating his narrowness, democratic liberty will continue to receive the critics' scorn.

Beyond Practical Virtue

Fortunately, there is hope for individual development under democracy. Although the democratic struggle indeed fails to call forth *directly* many of the higher virtues (wisdom, an appreciation of beauty, and so forth), and though it breeds a certain arrogance in those who succeed in achieving autonomy, it nonetheless develops people more fully than other sociopolitical systems do. The democrat, because she is faced with challenges in all aspects of her life (a consequence of being isolated from a paternalistic hierarchy), tests and cultivates a wide range of abilities. The narrowness critics perceive is in fact less serious than it appears. To be sure, the typical democrat, actively engaged in the world, may not be fluent in Kantian metaphysics, but the abilities she *has* acquired can serve as the basis for fuller, broader development (which, depending on the particular person, might include a greater love of philosophy). Whereas in the next chapter I discuss the role of the democratic public sphere in achieving this end, in this section I focus on how the abilities democrats gain through their struggles prod them to recognize the larger meaning of the world around them.

In a world without protective, organic hierarchies, democrats must build their own social institutions. They must provide food for themselves and their families, by farming or earning wages. They must pay the bills, mow the lawn, feed the pets, care for the children—all tasks aristocrats would delegate to subordinates. This continual struggle for control of their destiny also requires that they increase the efficiency of their actions, thus turning their minds to the invention of labor-saving devices. (It is no coincidence that the American region noted for "Yankee ingenuity" is marked by both democratic institutions and a less-than-genial environment.)

The fact that one could expand the list of tasks that democrats complete for themselves almost indefinitely demonstrates that the forces under democracy that trigger individual development are varied and numerous—and certainly more numerous and varied than under aristocracy, where servants handle the daily chores of their masters. As a result, the excellence that arises from the democratic struggle, though perhaps narrow with respect to virtue entire, is plenteous and manifold with respect to practical virtue. In addition, such full practical excellence, by giving the democrat insight into the workings of her surroundings, naturally prepares her for a broader experience of the world.

For example, by devising more efficient tools for achieving mastery over nature, an inventor can gain a fairly sophisticated understanding of physical and chemical laws. Twain's Hank Morgan boasts that he has learned so much as a factory foreman about the practical workings of the world that he is able to "make anything a body wanted—anything in the world, it didn't make any difference what; and if there wasn't any quick new-fangled way to make a thing, I could invent one—and do it as easy as rolling off a log" (*CY* 4–5). Though his knowledge is primarily practical, it impinges upon the theoretical—even the highest levels of theory. Cooper's description of Andries Coejemans in *The Chainbearer* underscores this point;

though a common surveyor with little formal education, Coejemans has acquired through extensive practical experience an understanding of mechanics that is "better, perhaps, than if he had been a first-rate mathematician." Coejemans's practical experience yields wisdom that transcends mere instrumental knowledge, a fact that enables him to command the respect of his fellow villagers without cajoling or manipulating them (CB 299). Possessing such a deep common-sense understanding of applied science, as Hank and Coejemans do, requires a certain degree of contemplation about the overarching, unifying order of the physical world. Of course, this contemplation is initially for the sake of practical action, but it at least opens the door to an appreciation of higher truths—what Matthew Arnold would term "light."

Tocqueville argues that "democratic man likes generalizations because they save the trouble of studying particular cases . . . and contain . . . a lot in a small space and give a great return quickly." Democrats cease their inquiry when they have discovered a "common link" between phenomena, since further investigation would be a waste of valuable time. However, Tocqueville underestimates the degree to which democrats—especially in modern industrial societies—find deep practical knowledge useful in their daily lives. A superficial appreciation of patterns is rarely sufficient in an age that has seen the mechanization and rationalization of many key areas of life. With deep practical knowledge comes an unusually advanced appreciation of "common links" and their complexity.[12]

Just as practical science can give way to a greater theoretical understanding of the universe, certain daily tasks can themselves open one's mind to the greater significance of one's surroundings. Even the most uneducated, unrefined farmer, who has nothing on his mind but feeding his family and making a profit, is likely to appreciate the beauty of gently swaying corn tassels and the sweet scent of freshly mown hay. Though he may not be able to articulate his sensations in words, *he cannot help but notice* such magnificence, placed as he is in direct contact with nature. In addition, his appreciation is not merely that of a spectator who views from an aristocratic distance. The democratic farmer sees something greater in his fields, since they represent the workings of both himself and nature. The crops are not

12. Tocqueville, *Democracy,* 440.

only pleasant to look at, as they wave in the wind, but they exhibit a deeper beauty to him who planted and cultivated them. We should not forget the close link between *farming*, which cultivates the plants of the earth to produce a material good, food; and *gardening*, which uses the same techniques for a more elevated purpose: the production of beauty.

Parenting is yet another aspect of democratic life that pushes people to consider the higher aspects of existence. Being actively involved in a child's rearing, which requires an inordinate amount of time and energy, not only gives parents greater insight into the characteristics of human development, but makes them appreciate more directly the miraculous beauty of life. If, to maintain a life of leisure, parents were to delegate the major child-raising responsibilities to servants (as in aristocratic regimes), their appreciation of their children would be shallower and more distant. They would still experience a sensation of beauty, but it would be more akin to the emotion felt by an observer contemplating the splendor of someone else's fields. The responsibility that comes with democratic self-rule actually facilitates and deepens the experience of many forms of beauty—all of which work to expand the democrat's mind and character.

Cooper and Howells nicely capture the nuances of this relationship between democrats and nature. Though bent on destroying entire forests, Cooper's Billy Kirby makes a point of chopping down the noblest trees first. Though he does this mainly to demonstrate his superiority over nature, in seeking an adversary whose defeat will justify his arrogance he begins to see nature as something more than an object to control. The world comes to have qualities apart from its profitability.[13] Kirby's mind, like the farmer's, begins to transcend narrow practicality. Howells's Silas Lapham exhibits this same characteristic in a world more familiar to us. Though on the surface a single-minded capitalist, Silas is in fact driven not simply (and perhaps not even significantly) by greed, but rather by the pride he takes in creating a quality paint. Though we cringe at his bourgeois excesses and bad taste, there remains at his core something laudable, something that makes him—like Dryfoos and Kirby—more complicated than the critics would like to believe. Silas's paint, like the farmer's crops, is indeed bringing him material comfort, but in being produced it also inspires his high-

---

13. As Roderick Nash points out, "Cooper indirectly dignified wilderness by deprecating those insensitive to its ethical and aesthetic values." Nash, *Wilderness and the American Mind*, 76.

er sentiments—especially since he views himself as an active participant in the beautification of the world. A fresh coat of paint may not be the essence of beauty, but the elevated pleasure Silas experiences in creating his paint demonstrates that he appreciates more than mere creature comfort. As Van Wyck Brooks puts it, "Silas is a poet whose paint is a sentiment, a passion."[14] Like most producers of goods and services, Silas sincerely believes he is making the world a better place, not just lining his pockets. It is this sentiment, which often hides beneath the surface and escapes the critic's eye, that can serve as the foundation for fuller individual development (*SL* 16–17).

One of the most important ways in which democracy pushes people beyond the practical virtues is in the sphere of politics itself. Democracy implies that the people rule by laws and through institutions they have created. Polis building is necessitated not just by a social or political impulse within human nature, but by the fact that autonomy from the demands of nature can be achieved more easily as a team. Hank Morgan, Billy Kirby, and Jacob Dryfoos aside, most people need the support of a community to face the demands of a harsh world. By struggling in common for mastery over their environment, democratic citizens can achieve more as a group than each could achieve on his own.

However, through this collective struggle democrats accomplish something more than autonomy. By actively shaping and ruling their community, they tend to gain greater insight into the workings of the economic, social, and political worlds. Initially, this knowledge rises only to the level of common-sense precepts and rules of thumb, gained from frequent observation and reflection. However, as people work to improve their community, they begin to consider deeper questions. In the spirit of progress and efficiency (values that arise from the struggle with nature), democrats will tend to look to other communities for ideas on how to improve their own polity. This process of comparison and evaluation is valuable not only for the beneficial effects it has on civic virtue and the community's wellbeing, but also for how it broadens people's minds in general. Once citizens come to realize that significant differences exist among polities, they (as legislators for their own community) will begin to make conscious choices among possible policy alternatives. Even if a community's only

14. Van Wyck Brooks, *Howells: His Life and World,* 161.

thought is to increase its own productivity, safety, or justice, the very act of choosing priorities requires an examination of core political beliefs. For instance, to increase productivity citizens must first decide what productivity *is*, what values it includes and excludes, and why it might be an important good. Thinking in this way leads to a consideration of more abstract questions, such as why certain goods should be given priority over others. This process can become accelerated if surrounding communities rank goods in a different manner than one's own (for example, giving priority to civic virtue over wealth production). Rejecting these other systems, even if solely in the name of sheer practicality, requires engaging fundamental questions of human existence.

In sum, though the critics argue that a practical outlook prevents people from appreciating beauty and higher truths, they disregard the way in which practical experience prepares people for such a broader view of the world. The line separating practical virtue from a more refined sensibility is fuzzier than is commonly thought, and as we have seen, some of the most practical of experiences—those actions that are least beautiful in the critics' eyes (inventing, farming, paint manufacturing)—can be extraordinarily elevating to the soul. Of course, many of the higher sensations democrats experience are fleeting and left unarticulated, but they occur because the democratic struggle places people in a unique relationship with their environment—one in which their practical experience makes them receptive to wider meaning. What matters for the purpose of individual development is not what a given person is doing, but rather the meaning he attaches to his work. For Silas, producing paint not only earns him money, but is an expression of his higher instincts, in this case the desire to make the world a better, more beautiful place. Such sentiments may be found just as easily among modern "dot-commers," who rarely do what they do *solely* to retire at age forty. The impulse toward wealth-gathering is almost always intertwined with more laudable impulses in any given person, which means pulling democrats out of their supposed narrow practicality is not as difficult as the critics believe, and can be achieved in the presence of a healthy public sphere.

In reply to the critics' claim that liberal democracy, unlike hierarchical societies, contains no force that can elevate people out of narrow materialism, Cooper, Twain, and Howells demonstrate that the actual experience of living under conditions of equality and liberty has an elevating influence on one's character. Although the abilities that are called forth in this democratic struggle for autonomy are chiefly practical in nature, making democratic development at first seem narrow and stunted, in fact they open the door to fuller, richer development, by deeply engaging the democrat with her surroundings.

The fact that this development can take place in the absence of an aristocratic overclass (Carlyle, Nietzsche) or a state that actively cultivates certain ideals (Arnold, Mill) makes it more genuine and more just. It is genuine in the sense that the individual is in charge of her own destiny, and makes the decisions that guide her own development. If she were part of a hierarchy, her development would be contingent upon the wishes of her social superiors. She would indeed cultivate her talents, but out of fear, feudal duty, or deference to a privileged clerisy. If liberated from such controlling environments, she would no longer be motivated to maintain her level of development.

Democratic development is also more consistent with justice. The critics wish to use an aristocracy or an elite-guided state to preserve high ideals from the corrupting influence of the common people and their petty materialism. What they overlook, however, is the fact that democrats, though perhaps less refined than leisured aristocrats, are capable of greater development than given credit for; even if the critics are correct in asserting that they have made a poor showing to date, it is not because they are common by nature (and thus deserving of social or political subjection). They need the elevating influence of a vigorous public sphere to bring out their higher sensibilities. Once they enjoy these fundamental necessities, they can exhibit their own developmental strengths, such as a deeper, more direct sense of beauty and truth, gained through practical experience in the world. This will be the subject of the next chapter.

4

Individual Development and the Public Sphere

AT THIS POINT, the raw result of the democratic struggle confronts us: a narrow-minded arrogance arising from the anxious pursuit of material comfort in an unfriendly world. The arrogant materialist takes great pride in his conquest of nature, proving his superiority to his environment through wastefulness, conspicuous consumption,[1] and the like. In this respect, he deserves much of the criticism Carlyle and the other aesthetic critics heap upon him. Yet we have also seen that in struggling for autonomy, the democrat comes to see his surroundings as something more than an object of mastery. In grappling for a degree of security and comfort, he gains a grudging respect for his environment and recognizes its inherent nobility. This crude appreciation of the world and its inhabitants, born of the democratic struggle for autonomy, is the vital force behind individual development within democracy. What we need is a refinement mechanism that can restrain democratic arrogance and materialism while nourishing and elevating the nobler sentiments the democratic struggle calls forth.

In this chapter, I investigate the effects of the democratic public sphere

---

1. *Conspicuous consumption* is Thorstein Veblen's term. In *The Theory of the Leisure Class,* Veblen maintains that "[i]n order to be reputable, [consumption] must be wasteful. No merit would accrue from the consumption of the bare necessities of life, except by comparison with the abjectly poor who fall short even of the subsistence minimum" (60). For example, one of Cooper's characters in *Homeward Bound,* a staunch democrat, uses stolen money to buy thirty-six pairs of pants (*HB* 562).

on individual development. With the novelists' assistance, I show how democratic interaction contributes to individual development by helping people make sense of their struggle with nature, giving them added perspective on the questions confronting them, encouraging them to moderate and qualify their opinions, and inculcating habits of fair and open discourse. Before developing these points, however, we must discuss the nature of the democratic public sphere—in other words, the specific way in which liberty and equality characterize interpersonal relations in a democracy.

The Public Sphere and Democratic Deliberation

When Aristotle wrote that man is a political animal by nature, he meant that we have the unique ability to express, through speech, our ideas of the expedient and the just. Unlike other animals, whose associations are based simply on biological need, we structure our associations around common conceptions of justice and the good life, arrived at through public deliberation. Since each person's views are likely to be at least partially true, the polis is best served by maintaining a public sphere in which each citizen can participate fully.[2]

Something akin to Aristotle's intuition is at the root of modern theories of the democratic public sphere, which emphasize full and fair participation in communal deliberation. In this section, I describe two common interpretations of the public sphere's role in democratic society: one concerned with legitimacy and justice, the other with the effects of common deliberation on the character of the participants. In the process, I will demonstrate how my work differs from and draws upon these conceptions.

Although Jürgen Habermas may not be the father of deliberative democracy (John Stuart Mill, the Enlightenment philosophes, or even Aristotle might have a better claim to that title), he is undeniably its most powerful contemporary defender. For him, following Weber, the problem of the modern world lies in its "disenchantment," the fact that religious and metaphysical justifications of social norms are no longer widely accepted. No longer can we appeal to God or unquestioned rational standards to justify

---

2. Aristotle, *Politics,* bk. 1, chap. 2, 1253a. For some of Aristotle's arguments in favor of the many, see bk. 3, chap. 15, 1286a22–b1.

our social practices; we must ground legitimacy elsewhere. Letting each community choose its own norms is one option, but the necessary unification of state and people under such a republican scheme remains troubling (Robespierre, Mussolini, and Hitler come to mind). In the interest, then, of obtaining reasonable or fair results while preserving the legitimacy associated with democratic will-formation, Habermas offers a theory of justice grounded in discourse, well summarized in the following principle: "Just those action norms are valid to which all possibly affected persons could agree as participants in rational discourses." Much of Habermas's work is consequently devoted to understanding the preconditions and procedures for rational discourse, and how the resultant norms gain legitimacy.[3]

The idea that the public sphere is an arena for deliberating about justice, and that the results of full and fair discourse can be considered legitimate, is common among modern theorists. John Rawls, for example, argues in *Political Liberalism* that reasonable disagreement about the ends of human life is inescapable in a society devoted to liberty. To achieve stability amidst such diversity of comprehensive worldviews, we need a "political conception of justice that all citizens might be reasonably expected to endorse," an "overlapping consensus" that "consists of all the reasonable opposing religious, philosophical, and moral doctrines likely to persist over generations and to gain a sizable body of adherents in a more or less just constitutional regime." Rawls believes a conception of "justice as fairness" will attract such a consensus, but emphasizes that any consensus arises from discussion and is always subject to further examination: in the realm of civil society, "we as citizens discuss how justice as fairness is to be formulated, and whether this or that aspect of it seems acceptable—for example, whether the details of the set-up of the original position are properly laid out and whether the principles selected are to be endorsed." The reasonableness of the consensus, as well as its legitimacy, is grounded in its conformity to our considered convictions about justice. Rawls criticizes Habermas for viewing the results of ideal deliberation as objectively true, but the two thinkers are on common ground in emphasizing the primacy of public debate in establishing legitimate standards of justice.[4]

3. Jürgen Habermas, *Between Facts and Norms,* 71, 107, 295–302.
4. Rawls, *Political Liberalism,* 3–4, 15, 133, 137, 380–85, 383n14.

Most critics of Habermas and Rawls accept the idea that free and open public discourse will contribute to a durable system of justice; their main concerns are with defining the nature and procedures of that discourse. Feminist theorists, for example, call attention to the masculine bias inherent in defending positions with reference to principles rationally acceptable by all. Communitarians, meanwhile, take issue with Rawls for downplaying the importance of overall conceptions of the good life in deliberating about justice, and Michel Foucault reminds us that even the "freest" and most "open" discourses are fraught with subtle power imbalances. Despite these objections, however, the critics generally agree that discourse, provided it is conducted in a satisfactory manner, could yield legitimate principles of justice.[5]

The second line of inquiry concerns the effects of a vibrant public sphere on citizens' character. In his travels through the United States, Tocqueville noted that Americans' propensity to form political and civil associations offsets their tendency toward individualism. Unlike despotism, democracy compels people to take an interest in public affairs, to "turn from the private interests and occasionally take a look at something other than themselves." When the administration of minor affairs is decentralized to local districts, residents "are always meeting, and they are forced, in a manner, to know and adapt themselves to one another." The relationship between political and civil associations is key: "It is through political associations that Americans of every station, outlook, and age day by day acquire a general taste for association and get familiar with the way to use the same. Through them large numbers see, speak, listen, and stimulate each other to carry out all sorts of undertakings in common. Then they carry these conceptions with them into the affairs of civil life and put them to a thousand uses." Associations prevent people from being "shut up in the solitude of [their] own heart[s]" by showing them the myriad ways in which they are dependent upon each other. By participating in an association—even

5. Examples of the feminist critique include Iris Marion Young, "Communication and the Other: Beyond Deliberative Democracy," in Seyla Benhabib, ed., *Democracy and Difference;* and Maria Pia Lara, *Moral Textures.* For the communitarian critique, see Sandel, *Liberalism;* MacIntyre, *After Virtue;* and Walzer, *Spheres of Justice.* For Foucault's views, see Michel Foucault, *Discipline and Punish.* My interpretation of Foucault's attitude toward deliberative democracy follows James Johnson, "Comment" on "Public Sphere, Postmodernism and Polemic."

a relatively trivial one—isolated individuals become aware of the link between their private interest and the common good, and they take on the character of active citizens. Collaborating with one's neighbors within democratic institutions advances justice and the common good in a tangible fashion, by creating "social capital," but it also reorients one's soul. According to Tocqueville, this transformation is vital to the continuing success of democracy, both in America and abroad.[6]

Robert Bellah and his coauthors of *Habits of the Heart,* like Tocqueville, are concerned with the actual effects of democratic institutions on the development of civic duty. Though painfully aware of the forces (urbanization, industrialization, social mobility) that encourage individualism and undermine the democratic public sphere, these authors affirm Tocqueville's insight that democratic participation can bring fulfillment to those involved. Vestiges of the civic sense that participation cultivates is evident among "town fathers"—those citizens who come to identify their own interests with their community's, initially through careful calculation, but eventually through instinct. Habituating themselves to public participation (by planning a parade or joining the Rotary Club) brings a certain joy or "fun"; they contribute enthusiastically, without coercion. In the process, their character is transformed.[7]

Of course, modern industrial society, coupled with administrative centralization, is largely anathema to the kind of direct participation that encourages civic-mindedness. Yet this should not prevent us from considering the relationship between democratic institutions and civic development, just as the presence of power inequalities in actual life does not hinder Habermas from outlining the conditions of an ideal speech situation. The first step is to identify the link between free institutions and civic virtue; whether we can preserve or create such institutions is a separate question.

My own project is allied more closely to Tocqueville's and Bellah's. Unlike Rawls and Habermas, my primary concern is not with establishing legitimate principles of justice, but with determining the effects of democ-

6. Tocqueville, *Democracy,* 508, 510–11, 524. On social capital, see Robert Putnam, *Bowling Alone.*

7. Robert Bellah et al., *Habits of the Heart,* esp. chap. 7. For a discussion of the political consequences of "democratic talk," see Benjamin Barber, *Strong Democracy,* chap. 7.

racy on citizens' development. However, Habermas's and Rawls's discussions of fair deliberative procedures are central to an understanding of what makes institutions democratic—a necessary precondition for determining their influence on citizens. Unlike Tocqueville and his followers, my interest is not just in the development of civic duty or habits of political participation, but in individual development as a whole. I argue that interacting with other citizens in a democratic public sphere not only prompts devotion to the regime, but elevates one's character and sentiments in a much broader sense.

Because I am concerned with the wider effects of democratic life on the individual, it makes sense to define the public realm expansively, as Tocqueville does. What is interesting about his study of associations is the way in which he views the activities of everyday life as part of the public sphere. Though most associations are not explicitly political, all (or nearly all) involve the voluntary participation of equal individuals in the pursuit of a common good. Their actions are public in much the same sense as legislative acts are public: they are the results of common deliberation within a framework largely void of formal inequalities. Once we look beyond the question of justification/legitimation, we can appreciate democracy's pervasive influence on citizens' development. Daily interaction under conditions of freedom and equality lends itself well to the participants' overall development.

However, not everything discussed or pursued in common by democrats is political or aimed at a concrete good; to get at the wider implications of democratic interaction, we need to elaborate upon Tocqueville's insight. Here the novelists can again be of service. They provide us with detailed accounts of how democratic people interact with each other, how they view themselves and their neighbors, what attitudes and ideas they bring to discussion, and how democratic interaction transforms them. With their help, we can better understand how democratic institutions and the everyday habits of democrats contribute to individual flourishing.

In defining the expanded public realm, we should include not only legislative sessions, town hall meetings, and the judicial system, but also the other interactions that democracy makes "public," such as two neighbors chatting over their backyard fence, friends meeting for coffee, or a dinner party. In essence, any time people approach each other freely and on equal standing, to discuss what they deem important, a similar end is accomplished. This is because nearly every interpersonal relationship under democracy is marked, in theory, by the same basic characteristics. Specifically, each participant, as a citizen of the regime, has something valuable to contribute to the discussion, be it desire-based preferences or carefully reasoned arguments. Since no political superior exists who can legitimately suppress such ideas, each person can reasonably expect the other participants to hear him out. On the other hand, since he is only the equal of his fellows, never their superior, he cannot dismiss their remarks as casually as he could those of an inferior. (Of course, we can always reject whatever we please, but it is nonetheless clear that the norms of democracy encourage us, more than any other regime, to listen respectfully to others.)

Even family relationships become more egalitarian under liberal democracy, making the interaction of husband and wife somewhat analogous to the broader public sphere. Spouses treat each other as equal partners, confiding more deeply in each other as paternalistic traditions pass away, and transforming themselves in the process. A significant aspect of Silas Lapham's moral regeneration, for example, involves his reunion with his wife, Persis, whom, though instrumental to his early success, he had excluded from many of his subsequent business decisions. Now, after a series of reverses, Silas realizes his mistake and opens up to Persis. In the midst of their despair, they "fell asleep . . . talking hopefully of his affairs, which he laid before her fully, as he used to do when he first started in business. That brought the old times back" (*SL* 278–79). With Persis's help, Silas comes to see the importance of balancing the demands of the marketplace against the dictates of conscience, and decides to reject the underhanded deal that would have saved his business.

The democratic marriage relationship is just one of many informal, everyday arenas for the sort of communication that improves participants' character and outlook. A society in which people can express and defend their ideas without fear, where a person's social rank is irrelevant in determining the quality of his ideas, is peculiarly conducive to fuller individual development. Howells's Jacob Dryfoos and Silas Lapham, for example, by participating in democratic discussion, are able to retain what is valuable in their capitalist outlook while gradually being influenced by value systems at odds with their own. In democratic discussion, each view is privileged only by its own persuasiveness, which means that Dryfoos need not defer entirely to the socialist Lindau, nor Lapham to the aristocratic Bromfield Corey, unless they find something intrinsically valuable in their opponent's viewpoint. Dryfoos and Lapham become fuller individuals through democratic interaction not by abandoning their old selves, but by steadily revaluing their beliefs in the context of free and equal discussion.

One might object that the majority of common speech is not extraordinarily elevating, consisting largely of chitchat about the weather, movies, and the relative merits of Ford and Chevrolet (or is it now Honda and Toyota?), but the same is true of all societies that have nothing more pressing to discuss. When the stakes are high, democrats are just as serious as their counterparts in other regimes—and perhaps more so, given their responsibility as shapers of their collective destiny. One must not confuse the effects of peace and economic prosperity with those of democracy. Another potential objection is that those who possess rhetorical abilities or a booming voice will tend to dominate discussion, regardless of the actual worth of their contributions. Yet this problem is endemic to all regimes. At least democracy removes most formal and many informal inequalities, forcing even the cleverest speakers to defend their positions with plausible arguments, since their listeners will no longer defer to noble birth or divine right. Nor, importantly, is democracy a humorless regime. Having a democratic outlook depends on the ability to laugh at both ourselves and others. In this sense, Twain is the consummate democrat, making fun of humanity without exempting himself from ridicule.

How the Public Sphere Can Tame Arrogant Materialism

When functioning correctly, the democratic public sphere does a reasonably good job of identifying and filtering out cant, hypocrisy, and flawed arguments. Equality breeds a healthy skepticism, and the free interchange of ideas in such an atmosphere cannot fail to be productive. Of course, any existing democracy contains all sorts of countervailing tendencies, many of which derive from older regimes and traditions, a problem I address later in this chapter. For now, however, I will concentrate on the effects of a more ideal form of the democratic public sphere, where people can approach and communicate with each other freely and equally, and where arguments become accepted or rejected because of their intrinsic value, not the social or material resources of the speaker. Put differently, I will focus on the tendencies and effects of actual liberal democracy when it is working properly. Unlike Habermas and Rawls, I have no need to invoke a sanitized version of democracy.

From Intuition to Conscious Idea

The first and broadest of these effects is that we begin to make sense of our struggle with nature. What at first is only an intuition—for example, that the environment we struggle with is somehow endowed with meaning or nobility—becomes consciously articulated in conversation with others. Cooper may have romanticized Natty Bumppo's interaction with the natural world, but was shrewdly insightful in emphasizing his friendship with Chingachgook. It is precisely because Natty is not a solitary hermit that he is such a compelling character. His innate sense of justice and "fit" seems mystical and abstract—one might say nonhuman—as long as it remains on the level of intuition. His lifelong struggle with nature has flooded his senses with knowledge of the world, yet wisdom requires that he filter and organize this information for it to be of much human use. He must bring his reason and critical sensibilities to bear on this cacophony of impressions, a process that he can accomplish only imperfectly in isolation from other human beings. Thus, when Natty begins to discuss his intuitions with others, in particular Chingachgook, his thoughts become more ordered, more circumscribed, and more human than if he had remained alone. Of course, like most close friends, Natty and Chingachgook rarely need extended conversations to communicate their deepest thoughts (a knowing glance or a brief sentence is often enough), but this communication—in whatever form it takes—is vital to each man's pursuit of wisdom.

Cooper seems equally interested, however, in how Natty interacts with people other than Chingachgook—especially people who have had a dramatically different experience of the world, or who have risen only to the stage of arrogant materialism. In either case, Natty cannot expect his interlocutor to share his intuitions. As a result, he must articulate his ideas explicitly and logically. More subtle forms of communication may suffice between close friends, but most democratic interaction is between people who do not know each other in depth. Family, love, and war bind people together in a way that often makes the formal expression of opinions superfluous at best. The participants in such organic relationships know each other intimately, and through common experience share the same worldview. They feel the truth together; they need not explain it to each other.

When these organic relationships become institutionalized, this effect is even greater. For example, in Robert Filmer's patriarchal conception of political order, the king's duties to his people are analogous to the natural duties of a father, and the community's interests are assumed to cluster like those of a family. As a result, free and open discourse is unnecessary at best, and at worst dangerously subversive. Jean-Jacques Rousseau's civic republic, though not patriarchal, similarly downplays the role of deliberation. For Rousseau, "[s]o long as a number of men gathered together consider themselves as a single body, they have a single will also, which is directed to their common conservation and to the general welfare." In such a situation, "the common good is obvious everywhere, and all that is required to perceive it is good sense." Natty and Chingachgook, like the members of Rousseau's republic, possess an abundance of "good sense," which makes them capable of comprehending the good and the just without extensive deliberation with each other.[8]

Under modern liberal democracy, however, organic relationships, though still common, lack the institutional force they enjoy under other regimes. Whereas aristocracy "links everybody, from peasant to king, in one long chain," liberal democracy "breaks the chain and frees each link."[9] Democrats are alone in the world, which forces them to communicate with each other differently. In advancing an idea, one can no longer assume that the listener will automatically grant one's premises; in fact, it is likely that the listener will advance a worldview dramatically at odds with one's own. At first this hinders communication, and threatens to isolate people even further. However, the basic fact that people cannot fully make sense of their environment on their own drives them back together again.

What results is a form of critical dialogue, where freedom and equality govern discourse, and where ideas must be expressed in a manner accessi-

---

8. Robert Filmer, *Patriarcha and Other Writings;* Rousseau, *The Social Contract,* 134.
9. Tocqueville, *Democracy,* 508.

ble to people with diverse outlooks. The necessity of communicating in this way forces democrats to think much more carefully about the sensory impressions they receive from their environment, since they must organize their thoughts more completely to communicate them effectively. In this respect, conversation between close friends is much easier than that between two citizens who are strangers, for the latter begin with less in common. This is not to say that dialogue between two friends will not bring out the best in each of them, but rather that democratic discourse itself powerfully drives critical reflection (that is, it exercises an independent causal force).

We see this vividly in *The Deerslayer*. Natty's experiences in the woods have enhanced both his resourcefulness and his sense of nature's majesty, but the former has never really been tested, and the latter remains an intuition, not a fully conscious idea. In the course of the novel, Natty comes to prove himself as a warrior, but for our purposes, his more interesting progress is in the realm of thought. At first, he is idealistic in an *immediate* way; he receives truths from nature directly, without having them explained to him, or having to explain them to others. As the book develops, though, Natty's almost subconscious worldview comes into conflict with the values of Tom Hutter and Harry March, who wish to attack a Huron encampment to procure scalps for sale to the British. Natty recoils at the thought of killing people for money, but Tom and Harry advance seemingly compelling arguments in favor of their plan. Tom notes that "high prices are offered for scalps on both sides," and that "when mankind is busy in killing one another, there can be no great harm in adding a little bit of skin to the plunder." Harry agrees, arguing that though "with *white* people 'tis different, for they've a nat'ral avarsion to being scalped, . . . your Indian shaves his head in readiness for the knife and leaves a lock of hair by way of braggadocio that one can lay hold of in the bargain" (*DS* 42).

Natty's task is a difficult one, since to convince Tom and Harry that higher principles should govern war and conquest, he must articulate those principles in a way that they can understand. Tom (a former buccaneer) and Harry (an uncouth man of the settlements) have not experienced the world in the same way Natty has, and they are blind to the greater significance of their surroundings. To change their minds, Natty must provide a decent rebuttal to their arguments, which requires him first to understand his own feelings. His first attempt at articulating his opposition, "I'll not unhumanize my natur' by falling into ways that God intended for another race," is rather weak, and open to Harry's wry counterargument that since the Hurons scalp the English and their Indian allies, "one good turn desarves another." However, Natty gradually comes into his own, subjecting his intuitions to critical examination and organizing them in a way that directly addresses Tom's and Harry's concerns. Christian doctrine requires that we turn the other cheek, he argues, and forgiveness—not revenge—is the white man's gift. Harry scoffs at this answer, believing it a hopelessly naive doctrine, but Natty gains the upper hand: "Don't mistake me, March," he replies, "I don't understand by this any more than that it's *best* to do this, if *possible*. . . . Overlook all you *can* is what's meant; and not *revenge* all you can." Natty notes that Harry interprets the relevant ethical ideal as "do as you're done by," when in fact the proper (and eminently practical) ideal is "do as you *would* be done by" (*DS* 42–44).

By articulating his moral and aesthetic principles, Natty becomes a more conscious being, capable of reflecting critically on his intuitions. One might even say that his friendship with Chingachgook—though based on deep affinity and shared intuition—does less to make him fully conscious than his debates with the narrow-minded settlers. The latter force him to order his thoughts, rein in his emotions, and make sense of the flow of information that comes to him from nature. In contrast, since Chingachgook and he are of one mind (or as much as two people of different ethnic and social backgrounds can be), he can be satisfied with his intuitions. After all, they match Chingachgook's. He has no need to think through his convictions in the context of that friendship. To be sure, he talks with Chingachgook about the differing "gifts" and traditions of the two races (*LM* chap. 2), but there is no doubt that the prominent feature of their relationship is similarity, not difference. There is not enough difference between the two men to spur the critical thinking necessary for fuller human development.

The young Natty is like an artist who never paints anything, or a philosopher who never expounds his philosophy: he has insight, but little real understanding. The process of writing one's thoughts down on paper, representing them on canvas or in clay, or expressing them in speech forces one to come to terms with those thoughts. (The Greek word *logos,* which connotes both reason and speech, nicely captures the close link between understanding something and being able to express it to others.)[10] The most obvious theme of *The Deerslayer*, Natty's progression from hunter to warrior, recedes in importance as we see him develop into a conscious being, having gained a better understanding of himself and his surroundings by explaining himself to people unlike himself. This process is hardly over at the end of *The Deerslayer*, for even as an old man in *The Pioneers* and *The Prairie* Natty struggles to explain himself to his countrymen (a problem Cooper himself had). Yet it is this struggle, this challenge to make ourselves clear to others, that compels us to reflect more carefully on ourselves and the information that flows through our senses.

Liberal democracy singularly conduces to this sort of activity, by respecting diversity, grounding discourse in freedom and equality, and orienting everyone—not just a select few—toward their environment in a way that generates insightful thoughts in the first place. The first guarantees a need for discussion, in that people disagree; the second ensures that people defend their positions with full and fair explanations, not with force or appeals to one's social status; while the third, by making it possible for everyone to experience life in a relatively unmediated fashion, guarantees a supply of ideas to discuss. What is true for Natty Bumppo, Mozart, Michelangelo, and others of unusual insight is, under democracy, essentially true (albeit to a lesser degree) for all people. At the very least, there is less to hinder people's pursuit of wisdom than in hierarchical societies and, as I demonstrated in Chapter 3, democracy actually tends to elevate people beyond narrow, materialistic viewpoints.

Gaining Perspective

The second effect of the democratic public sphere is to prompt people to view their initial opinions from the perspective of others. Whereas the preceding discussion focused on how democracy encourages people to bring order to their muddled masses of emotions and insights, so that they can explain themselves to others, this section concerns how those initial explanations become tested in public discussion, and how we acquire a bet-

---

10. For the most famous use of *logos* as "speech," see Aristotle, *Politics*, bk. 1, chap. 2, 1253a10.

ter vantage point for understanding ourselves as a result. In the earlier stage, perspective (the distancing necessary for making sense of our insights) is provided by our own mind, and is consequently quite limited. Only geniuses—if anyone—can achieve understanding solely within their own minds, with limited human contact. For everyone else, it is necessary to proceed to the second phase of democratic interaction, where we gain critical perspective by submitting our ideas to public scrutiny.

In *A Hazard of New Fortunes,* Howells masterfully depicts Jacob Dryfoos's encounter with foreign ideas. Dryfoos is confident in the worth of his own opinions, and feels comfortable expressing them. He knows what he is about—or at least he thinks he does. In his rise to wealth, he has come to value hard work, responsibility, and cleverness, and he considers himself dedicated to the common good. During the Civil War, he was an active recruiter of volunteers, paying bounties out of his own pocket. Though as a father of young children he did not serve in the army, he supported his substitute's family after the war. He is motivated by a worldview that has a sort of nobility about it, though it is not as elevated or mystical as Natty Bumppo's. In the course of his struggle to the top, Dryfoos has begun to learn that the meaning of life cannot be reduced to material comfort; for example, his patriotism and his desire to see his daughters admitted to New York society counterbalance his love of money. Basil March notes that Dryfoos is racked with guilt for sitting out the Civil War, and perceives a "dormant nobleness in the man." By the time we meet Dryfoos in *A Hazard,* he has already progressed through the first stage of public participation, having gained enough perspective on his inner values to explain them in public. What Howells focuses on, however, is how far Dryfoos still needs to go to gain a full understanding of himself and his social environment—and how active dialogue with others can serve to liberate him from his original perspective (*HNF* 274, 290–91).

The primary device Howells uses to illustrate Dryfoos's shortcomings is the dinner party, where people of varying backgrounds and outlooks gather together in conversation. Though a bit contrived, the dinner party scene in *A Hazard* is roughly analogous to the types of discussion and debate that occur in more casual settings throughout democratic society. Dryfoos invites the staff of his literary journal to his home both to discuss matters pertaining to the journal and to display his wealth conspicuously. Among the guests are an artist (Beaton), a southern gentleman (Colonel Woodburn), a promoter (Fulkerson), the journal's editor (March), and a radical socialist (Lindau). As Fulkerson, the main proponent and organizer of the dinner, notes, "Dryfoos . . . thought he was doing all his invited guests a favor, and while he stood in a certain awe of them as people of much greater social experience than himself, regarded them with a kind of contempt as people who were going to have a better dinner at his house than they could ever afford to have at their own" (*HNF* 282). Dryfoos is convinced that he is just as worthy as any of his guests, and he intends to buy the only thing he lacks, social status, with parties such as this one.

The table discussion quickly veers into literature, as Lindau makes allusions to Shakespeare, Woodburn predictably extols the virtues of Scott and Addison, and Beaton praises Baudelaire. Meanwhile, "Dryfoos listened uneasily; he did not quite understand the allusions, though he knew what Shakespeare was, well enough." Knowing so little about literature that he cannot even appreciate its importance, he grows impatient. Fulkerson notices, and tries to steer the conversation back to personal stories. Finally Dryfoos is on familiar ground, and he tells of his experiences as a recruiter in 1861. He toasts Lindau, who lost an arm in the Union Army, for his valor, and agrees with Woodburn that honor, not greed, motivated southern soldiers (*HNF* 289–92).

However, the discussion takes a turn for the worse when Woodburn launches a full-scale assault on northern capitalism. Woodburn decries commercialism as "the poison at the heart of our national life," and argues that "the infernal impulse of competition" has taught us "to trick and betray and destroy one another in the strife for money, till now that impulse had exhausted itself, and we found competition gone, and the whole economic problem in the hands of monopolies." Lindau applauds the critique, as does Dryfoos—though with a wariness arising from his ignorance of the argument's real import: "Dryfoos tried to grasp the idea of commercialism as the Colonel seemed to hold it; he conceived of it as something like the dry-goods business on a vast scale, and he knew he had never been in that. He did not like to hear competition called infernal; he had always supposed it was something sacred, but he approved of what Colonel Woodburn said of the Standard Oil Company; it was all true; the Standard Oil had squeezed Dryfoos once and made him sell it a lot of oil wells." Unaware of the depth of Woodburn's argument, Dryfoos naively boasts of his ability to manage workers, of how he had cunningly broken a strike and arranged with his fellow capitalists to hire only non-union labor. Lindau is outraged by Dryfoos's anti-union stance, and calls him a traitor, *auf Deutsch*. Dryfoos is still bewildered, and the conversation quickly descends into an angry debate between Woodburn and Lindau over the best solution to the problem of capitalism. By the time everyone leaves, Dryfoos is fuming, furious that Lindau has ruined his celebratory dinner (*HNF* 292–300).

At this point, it is unclear whether Dryfoos has changed much. Judging from his subsequent behavior (the next morning he orders March to fire Lindau), he appears to have held stoutly to his beliefs. However, there seems to be a gradual shift in Dryfoos's character, hastened somewhat by Conrad's death. Howells is too much of a realist to make Dryfoos an entirely new man at the end of the novel, but he does emphasize certain alterations within Dryfoos's outlook, the result of his interchanges with Lindau, Conrad, and the other journal contributors. Dryfoos visits March again, this time to explain his rash behavior regarding Lindau. He points out that his Pennsylvania Dutch upbringing had enabled him to understand Lindau's insults. This was the real reason he had pressured March to fire him—not because he wanted to suppress his opinions as such. In fact, Dryfoos tries to show March how his business practices are worker-friendly: "I always done the square thing by my hands, and in that particular case out there [his breaking of a strike], I took on all the old hands just as fast they left the union. As for the game I came on them [bringing in replacement workers], it was dog-eat-dog anyway" (*HNF* 388–89).

March almost laughs to see Dryfoos respond to Lindau's critique in this manner, as if it were enough to treat laborers well, so long as they renounce their union. Upon reflection, though, March realizes that Dryfoos, despite the crudeness of his new sentiments, is at least on the path to fuller development. We cannot expect people to change suddenly, he argues, even when they experience cataclysmic events. The Puritan reformers were on to something, he continues, in proclaiming that "it is the still, small voice that the soul heeds, not the deafening blasts of doom." Conrad's death did not fundamentally transform Dryfoos; it "benumbed him, but couldn't change him." As March explains, "There's the making of several characters in each of us; we *are* each several characters, and sometimes this character has the lead in us, and sometimes that. From what Fulkerson has told me of Dryfoos I should say he had always had the potentiality of better things in him than he has ever been yet, and perhaps the time has come for the good to have its chance. The growth in one direction has stopped; it's begun in another; that's all" (*HNF* 422). Dryfoos has slowly been forced to evaluate himself by a standard other than wealth and social status, causing submerged elements of his character to rise to the surface. For too long he had been viewing life narrowly, strictly as a businessman would. Now, because of the persistent challenges of the democratic public sphere, he is becoming more fully developed and more fully human than before.

Perhaps in the end Dryfoos never completely understands Lindau's perspective, nor has he radically changed as a person, but interaction with others in a democratic setting has at least exposed him to viewpoints that challenge his own. In time, provided he continues to encounter different points of view, he might gradually come to see his life from a more balanced, sophisticated perspective. In this sense, Dryfoos is no different from anyone else; we are all so attached to our own partial interpretations of the truth that we find it exceedingly difficult to look at ourselves from another's vantage point. Yet Dryfoos's painful process of self-discovery, triggered by his encounters with Lindau, Woodburn, March, and the rest of the novel's characters, is also indicative of our own experience. More than any other regime, democracy holds out the promise that we can step outside ourselves and view ourselves critically, since we are constantly in contact with people who differ from us and hold opinions contrary to ours. (This is true even in relatively homogeneous societies, as long as there is enough diversity to require us to explain ourselves to each other.) This process is rarely smooth, stripped as it is of the moderating influences of aristocratic customs and manners; and it often works slowly (even imperceptibly); but it does work. To reject another's viewpoint we must first try to understand it (at least superficially). Living a life full of these encounters leads almost by necessity to our own development. If Howells is right that such a person as Dryfoos can change for the better within democracy, there is plenty of hope for the rest of us.

Opinion Qualification

The third effect of the democratic public sphere is to cause people to qualify their opinions in light of dissenting views. With Dryfoos, this process has just begun. He has reached the stage where he begins to understand other people's perspectives, and is almost paralyzed by the shock to his self-confidence. However, continued exposure to democratic discussion will help him move beyond this point. Within democratic conditions, we are more likely to accept part or all of what others are arguing, and to modify our own opinions accordingly. We come to qualify our overly bold positions, and expand our overly timid positions. Through discussion and interaction with others in a setting of freedom and equality, we begin to synthesize our insights with those of others, resulting in a deeper, more accurate understanding of the human condition.

Since in advancing an argument people are more apt to claim too much than too little, I will focus on how democracy causes overly bold positions to be qualified. The other situation, where arguments are not pressed as far as the evidence would allow (for example, a half-hearted legal defense or a tentative expression of one's preference for Beethoven over Mozart), is less relevant to this discussion. People are generally more likely to overstate their case than understate it, and this may be *the* fundamental political problem. Aristotle, for example, calls our attention to the partiality inherent in any claim to rule, and Hobbes makes us keenly aware of our proclivity toward vainglorious speech and action.[11] Our innate selfishness and our limited exposure to the world cause us to make bold, largely ignorant statements. Only when we come to have a wider experience of the world do we begin to moderate our views. Democracy is best able to give us this experience, by exposing us to different opinions within the context of free exchange.

Twain's *Connecticut Yankee in King Arthur's Court* illustrates this process of democratic opinion qualification. At the beginning of the tale, Hank Morgan is a confident, practical man, committed to material progress and republican government. By his own profession he is "nearly barren of sentiment . . . or poetry." Upon finding himself in sixth-century Britain, his first impulse is to put his nineteenth-century training to work in "bossing" the country into civilization. He is convinced of his intellectual and moral superiority, and much of the early part of the book is devoted to satirical observations on life in Camelot: how the noblewomen curse, how the Knights of the Round Table tell bald-faced lies while greasily munching

11. Aristotle, *Politics*, bk. 3, chap. 9; Hobbes, *Leviathan*, 125, chap. 13, esp. 184.

their supper, and how rats perch on King Arthur's head as he sleeps at the table. Hank sees little to commend in Camelot as it exists, and sets out to rid the nation of feudalism and superstition (*CY* 4, 11–17).

Given his democratic upbringing, Hank's first impressions are understandable. When confronted with feudal institutions, he sees them for what they are: a sham perpetrated by a tiny minority, aided by the Church, against the vast majority of the people. As I discussed in Chapter 2, even Camelot's "freemen" are de facto slaves, so degraded is their condition. Hank sticks to his principles, refuses to conform to prevailing norms of behavior, and successfully undermines the power of Merlin and the aristocracy. The victory of the nineteenth century's progressive spirit seems imminent. Yet in his single-minded pursuit of technological development and public re-education, Hank overlooks valuable aspects of the chivalric tradition. This becomes clear when he and Arthur tour the realm, disguised as peasants. Whereas Hank previously viewed Arthur as embodying the vices of aristocracy, he now comes to see him as possessing certain qualities of character superior to Yankee virtue.

Arthur's disguise cannot keep his spirit from showing through, despite Hank's best efforts to train the king to behave like a slave. After several close encounters, in which Arthur acts insufficiently subordinate, they arrive at a cottage whose inhabitants are dying of smallpox. Hank begs Arthur to leave immediately, lest he be exposed, but he insists upon helping: "Ye mean well," he tells Hank, "and ye speak not unwisely. But it were shame that a king should know fear, and shame that belted knight should withhold his hand where be such as need succor." Arthur carries a dying girl down from the loft to where her ailing mother is, causing Hank to observe: "Here was heroism at its last and loftiest possibility, its utmost summit; this was challenging death in the open field unarmed, with all the odds against the challenger, no reward set upon the contest, and no admiring world in silks and cloth of gold to gaze and applaud; and yet the king's bearing was as serenely brave as it had always been in those cheaper contests where knight meets knight in equal fight and clothed in protecting steel. He was great, now; sublimely great." Arthur's exhibition of pure courage puts Hank to shame. To be sure, Hank performs great deeds, but they are carefully calculated for effect and involve little bravery. Upon identifying the presence of smallpox, he had recoiled, knowing the potential costs of remaining in the vicinity.

Though common to Hank and other modern democrats, this sort of calculation and the self-interested attitude it rests upon is foreign to the
knightly code (*CY* 171–72).

In this sense, Arthur is more humane than his utilitarian companion,
and his deep humanity puzzles Hank. How can it be that such nobility of
character rises from the muck that is Camelot? In his review of *Connecticut Yankee,* Howells notes that "the mainly ridiculous Arthur of Mr.
Clemens has his moments of being as fine and high as the Arthur of Lord
Tennyson; and the keener light which shows his knights and ladies in their
childlike simplicity and their innocent coarseness throws all their best qualities into relief."[12] Hank's struggle to understand Arthur, with his mix of
desirable and undesirable traits, is one of the most interesting facets of the
book, and it illustrates the way in which democrats are able to synthesize
conflicting information.

It might seem strange that I use Hank Morgan's experiences as examples
of how the democratic public sphere functions. After all, despite his power within Camelot, Hank is still considered inferior to those of noble birth;
he never interacts with anyone on a free and equal footing. Hank was raised
a solid democrat, though, and democratic ideals guide his thought. On the
one hand, he exhibits a healthy skepticism, born of his conviction that no
man is inherently his superior. This makes it possible for him to see
Camelot as a sham and Arthur as a usurper of sovereign power. Rather than
being awed by demonstrations of knightly valor, he pokes fun at the vain-
glory, crudeness, and dullness that characterize the aristocracy of the kingdom. On the other hand, he realizes (though his pride often makes him
forget) that his own beliefs are equally subject to examination. He cannot
criticize Camelot in good faith unless he criticizes his own views as well.
After all, skepticism is only democratic if the skeptic exercises it toward
himself as well as others. This inward-looking skepticism is the result of being brought up democratically, and it enables Hank to reevaluate his priorities. Of course, it takes an experience as shocking as the smallpox scene
to jolt Hank out of his self-confidence, but democracy has at least made
him capable of synthesizing his original critical view of Arthur with his
newly sympathetic view.

12. William Dean Howells, "Editor's Study," 321.

Hank's democratic outlook gives him a more balanced view of things, for democracy has freed him of most dogmatism. He neither fawns before Arthur nor rejects him entirely. He sees him for what he really is: a flawed, rather dim man who exercises authority illegitimately, but often nobly. Without this democratic outlook, we would not be able to understand Arthur fully. We would see him as either Tennyson's idyllic king or a stupid man sleeping with a rat on his head. We would either be unwilling to consider his virtues (the attitude of those who consider themselves superior), or be blind to his vices (the attitude of the docile underling). The democrat is best able to see both sides of Arthur, and make a more accurate judgment of his character.

Democrats are not the only people capable of seeing both sides of an issue or all aspects of a phenomenon. However, they do enjoy the advantage of living under a regime that fosters the sort of investigation that draws upon multiple perspectives. Hank Morgan has been brought up in an atmosphere of free and open questioning, and exhibits a quintessentially democratic outlook—even when thrown into a hierarchical society. Rather than bow to the monarchy, he seeks to control it, confident in the value of his own opinions. Yet this confidence and self-aggrandizement is offset by his desire to institute a republic after Arthur's death, a sign that he knows his own tenure as The Boss is of questionable legitimacy. His blend of self-confidence and self-criticism in the context of social interaction is fundamentally democratic, and uniquely conducive to a fuller appreciation of the world.

Hank sometimes lets his self-confidence overwhelm his self-criticism, as in his arrogant challenge to the chivalry of England. Yet he emerges from his experience a more enlightened man. Having returned to the nineteenth century, he pokes fun at his old self and its lack of sentiment and poetry. As a factory boss, Hank had been "full of fight," and a crowbar blow to the head had been his time machine. But now he talks along "softly, pleasantly, flowingly," having tempered his keen, calculating Yankee spirit with a greater appreciation for a rival conception of the noble and good (*CY* 1, 4–5).

In *Connecticut Yankee,* Twain portrays a democratic man in an undemocratic setting. What is striking is how Hank develops as a person even though he does not interact with others who share his democratic values. In fact, someone raised within democracy can flourish outside democracy as long as he maintains an inner balance between self-confidence and self-criticism. Hank succeeds at this, and consequently is able to identify the most valuable elements of the Arthurian way of life and incorporate them into his own.

What is true of the democrat in an undemocratic setting is even truer in a democratic setting. Twain is careful, however, in speaking of America—especially the South—as a democracy. In *Life on the Mississippi,* he argues that the Civil War was caused in part by southerners' fanatical love of medieval romances: "[In the South,] the genuine and wholesome civilization of the nineteenth century is curiously confused and commingled with the Walter Scott Middle-Age sham civilization, as so you have practical common sense, progressive ideas, and progressive works, mixed up with the duel, the inflated speech, and the jejune romanticism of an absurd past that is dead, and out of charity ought to be buried." Furthermore, "it was [Scott] that created rank and caste down there, and also reverence for rank and caste, and pride and pleasure in them. Enough is laid on slavery, without fathering upon it these creations and contributions of Sir Walter." Southerners, despite having taken a leading role in founding the republic, were squandering their abilities on cheap romanticizations of a bygone era. Whereas Hank's confident attack on medieval practices makes his final estimate of medieval nobility more sober and accurate, southerners simply surrender their democratic skepticism, swooning before Scott's gilded heroes. They give in too easily to someone else's ideal, and in the process ruin their own civilization. Although Twain only hints at it, one could certainly argue that slavery's presence prompted the great affection for Scott's novels. Perhaps had slavery been abolished earlier, southerners might have been able to preserve their common sense and progressive temperament with few modifications. They would have seen through the "sillinesses and emptinesses, sham grandeurs, sham gauds, and sham chivalries" of a long-dead society, and would have embraced only those aspects of the medieval world that enhance understanding and inspire noble actions. Their fate would then have been similar to that of Hank, whose character remains largely intact, but softened and moderated by experience.[13]

13. Mark Twain, *Life on the Mississippi,* 375–76.

Habits of Democratic Interaction

The fourth main effect of the democratic public sphere is to instill habits of interaction that conduce to individual development. Whereas Tocqueville argues that active political participation draws democratic citizens out of individualism and makes them more likely to consider the common good, I shall make a broader case for democracy, one that points to the effects of democratic interaction on the whole person, not just the person qua citizen.

As noted earlier, similar forms of communication characterize a number of everyday democratic relationships. Neighbors, friends, husbands and wives, and even strangers communicate with each other more freely and equally under democracy than under other regimes. The result is that we are constantly placed in situations where we must craft our own ideas, articulate them to others, and respond generously to those who disagree with us. In democracy there are few places to escape from the burden of justifying one's actions—even for those who previously enjoyed a position of social superiority. For example, men can no longer tyrannize their wives and ignore their wishes, for the democratization of the family has ushered in the age of joint decision making. Though abuse still occurs, at least the abuser cannot invoke special legal privileges (for example, as the head of the patriarchal household).

Of course, not all relationships within democracy are equally democratic. Businesses are generally hierarchical, with most employees having little say in company management. In such an environment, a file clerk will enjoy less freedom of expression than a CEO and will tend to develop less as a person. Only in decentralized companies, where power is shared, will ordinary employees be likely to experience significant individual development. Otherwise, development will tend to occur only when workers are not working (for example, during lunch or coffee breaks, when they face their fellow workers as equals).

Yet something may be said even for hierarchical companies. An institution may be formally or informally democratic. A business, though often undemocratic in both a formal sense (as an instituted hierarchy of jobs and responsibilities) and an informal sense (as exhibiting a corporate culture that rewards deference), nonetheless can display certain formal and informal democratic traits. The most salient formal democratic characteristic is that employees in a market society consent to perform their jobs and are free to leave if dissatisfied, subject to restrictions. In addition, the fact that most employees are hired on the basis of merit, not family connections or bribery, further suggests that a strongly democratic bias is built into the structure of the modern corporation (and the capitalist system within which it operates). As far as informal democratic features are concerned, corporate cultures and leadership styles that encourage employee input and feedback help sustain democracy. A number of companies even allow their workers to dress casually, thereby removing one of the subtle customary barriers between employees of different ranks.

The result is that in nearly every part of our lives we are placed in situations where we must come to terms with our own intuitions, express our ideas to others in a frank, confident manner, and modify those ideas in the face of disagreement. Our relationships at work, at home, and in the community at large are all governed (some more than others) by the norms of democratic interaction, which instill in us the *habit* of interacting democratically. We get constant practice at explaining ourselves, listening to others, and reconciling discrepancies. We begin to act in ways that promote our own development almost without thinking about the process; it becomes second nature for us. Aristotle writes that a citizen is someone accustomed to ruling and being ruled in turn, and something akin to this notion is at work within democratic society as a whole. We come to realize that we have no monopoly on truth, and consequently operate under the assumption that talking with others will enhance our own understanding.

This is hardly a new idea, for Socrates advocated and lived according to it millennia ago. However, modern liberal democracy uniquely conduces to this sort of deliberation by essentially *requiring* it in all aspects of life. Unlike Athenian citizens, we have little choice but to live examined lives. The reward structure of our regime is such that it confers few benefits on those citizens who can neither think for themselves nor converse intelligently with others in life's various arenas. Athenian gentlemen only approached others as equals in the assembly, where the affairs of the polis were discussed; when not involved in politics, they went home and ordered about their families and slaves. We, in contrast, never really leave the assembly, as the different arenas of modern democratic life approach the assembly ideal in fundamental ways.

In *Connecticut Yankee,* Twain stresses the importance of habituating people to norms of democratic interaction. Hank succeeds in establishing man factories throughout Camelot, but the moment the Church places an interdict on him, his republican legions desert him. They had learned to act, speak, and reason as good democrats, but those behaviors had yet to become second nature for them. Hank's reforms had been superficial, hardly touching deep-rooted customs and superstitions; the culture within which Hank was trying to educate people was not, at base, amenable to democratic interaction. Once the Church reared its head, disrupting the fragile republic, Hank's democrats lost their nerve. They had worked to suppress their customary beliefs while in the man factories, but there was a limit to what they could accomplish, as long as they remained within a culture of superstition and deference. Thoroughly democratic institutions were necessary to support, sustain, and solidify their new democratic behaviors, and Hank's reforms had not yet achieved that end.

Cooper augments this understanding of democratic habit in *Homeward Bound,* a story of a voyage from England to the United States during which the passengers discuss and display characteristics of American life. Cooper contrasts two deficient forms of democratic habit (exhibited by Steadfast Dodge and Captain John Truck) in order to illustrate the habits that would result from truly democratic institutions. Dodge is an ardent New England democrat, committed to equality and suspicious of any practice that smacks of aristocracy (such as speaking privately behind closed doors). Dodge is so devoted to equality and the rights of the people that he has difficulty thinking for himself. His ambition is to be an ultra-democrat, a true "man of the people." In practice, however, his democratic enthusiasm undermines his individuality. He speaks or acts only if he is confident of the people's support; otherwise, he is afraid to draw attention to himself. As Cooper notes, "So much and so long had Mr. Dodge respired a moral atmosphere of this community-character, and gregarious propensity, that he had, in many things, lost all sense of his individuality; as much so, in fact, as if he breathed with a pair of county lungs, ate with a common mouth, drank from the town-pump, and slept in the open air." Dodge's vice is "a rabid desire for the good opinion of everything human, without always taking the means necessary to preserve his own"; he values others' judgments far above his own. Had he been raised in a truly liberal democratic community, he would have learned to defend his ideas, even in the face of communal disapproval, but it was not to be: Dodge, like Jason Newcome in *Satanstoe,* was brought up in a society that, though valuing democracy, taught its members to conform to communal religious and political standards. New England democracy, in Cooper's eye, was intrusive and deeply illiberal; it was also certainly destructive of any long-term development of individual capacities (*HB* 519–20).

Captain Truck, on the other hand, though also a New Englander, was raised to be fiercely independent. Having proven his abilities as a seaman, he had become the captain of a packet vessel, an office he performs with great skill. Unlike Dodge, Truck is "accustomed to rely on himself alone," and "was never more bent on following his own views than when all hands grumbled and opposed him." He knows that "every vessel must have a captain," and believes "mankind to be little better than asses." Whereas Dodge loses his individuality to the community, Truck tends to over-assert his. He is supremely confident of his talents, and accepts advice only from those of well-demonstrated ability. Decision is his greatest quality; seeking and taking counsel are not. Fortunately, "nature had made the possessor of so much self-will and temporary authority cool and sarcastic rather than hot-headed and violent." This radical individualism, nurtured by a lifetime of giving orders, is admirable in the person of Captain Truck (thanks to his cool nature), but it is nonetheless far from ideal. Put two Captain Trucks face to face, and they will talk past each other every time. Truck has not acquired the habit of listening; he has learned only to command. Had he been raised in a more balanced environment, he would have made a worse sea captain but unquestionably a better democrat (*HB* 520, 613).

Cooper's ideal is embodied better in Paul Powis, an American traveling under the pseudonym *Blunt.* Blunt maintains a better balance between self-confidence and deference than either Dodge or Truck. As a result, he is able to provide nuanced analyses of America's strengths and weaknesses, succumbing neither to the patriotic urge to defend the existing system at all costs nor to the impulse to harp on all of America's shortcomings. He applauds American ideals while admitting that their corresponding institutions often fail to restrain Americans' dangerous tendencies. He clearly has been raised to value what is best in both his own opinions and those of others, and he maintains this evenhanded approach almost by instinct, thanks to years of practice. Unlike Dodge and Truck, Blunt grew up in the Middle Atlantic region, which for Cooper was the only real seat of *liberal* democracy in America. In such a society, Blunt had received extensive experience in interacting with people on the basis of both freedom and equality. The result is a character oriented toward that type of behavior *by disposition,* and Blunt's development as a person is in no small way the consequence of this habituation (*HB* 525–26).

Twain and Howells are more cautious in advancing their visions of the well-developed citizen, but with a bit of triangulation we can understand their views on democratic habituation. For his part, Twain tends to emphasize two points: first, that habituation is an essential element in individual development, and second, that most people receive grossly imperfect training. As Hank Morgan observes, "[T]raining is everything; training is all there is *to* a person. We speak of nature; it is folly; there is no such thing as nature; what we call by that misleading name is merely heredity and training. We have no thoughts of our own, no opinions of our own; they are transmitted to us, trained into us. All that is original in us, and therefore fairly creditable or discreditable to us, can be covered up and hidden by the point of a cambric needle" (*CY* 91). The nobles and commoners of Camelot, the southerners of Twain's own time, and the vast majority of the human race meander through life confined by outdated, wrong-headed habits. Without the sort of thoroughgoing democratization Hank attempts to implement, or that Huck begins to experience in his friendship with Jim, people will continue to stifle their own humanity and good sense. They will continue to interact with each other not as fundamental equals, but as unthinking pieces of a dehumanized hierarchy. In the same vein of criticism, Howells argues that the habits of society types, self-made men, and social reformers are all skewed; by studying the shortcomings of existing habits of behavior, as in *The Rise of Silas Lapham* and *A Hazard of New Fortunes,* he shows how we can come to see how democratic interaction and individual development depend in the long run on certain habits, and how current institutions must be reformed in order to encourage those habits.

The Fragility of the Public Sphere

Now that I have outlined several laudable effects of the democratic public sphere on individual development, it is necessary to determine why, in real life, there is not always a direct correlation between the presence of formal democratic provisions, such as the rights to free speech and assembly, and actual individual development. What causes this disjunction? Are the critics correct in believing that democracy itself is to blame? In this section, I will point to features of existing liberal democracies that inhibit or corrupt the beneficial workings of the public sphere. Though many of these countervailing factors can, in principle, coexist with formal liberal democracy (and might even be seen as consequences of democracy), none are so inextricably linked to democracy as to prevent us from taking action against them on democratic grounds.

These detrimental effects fall into two categories: those that disrupt the peace and stability of a democratic community and those that undermine citizens' fellow feeling. The first category includes such events as physical harm, intimidation, violation of personal rights, and anything else that causes people to fear others within the community (fear of foreign aggression does not have the same detrimental effect). When a community's internal affairs become corrupted, the delicate balance between self-confidence and self-criticism, so vital to the success of democratic discussion and individual development, is upset. People either retreat in fear from public interaction or take advantage of others' uncertainty by zealously advancing their own interests. Twain points out the former tendency among the poor whites of the antebellum South, who submitted to the rule of the planters as willingly as Camelot's peasants bowed to their lords. Cooper describes a similar inclination among the law-abiding citizens of New York, who withdrew from public life in the face of radical democratic uprisings. The rebels took advantage of lax administration of the laws by successfully seizing and redistributing large estates, thereby intimidating their opposition out of the public realm. Like Twain's Morgan le Fay, they no longer felt compelled to listen to reason, having placed full confidence in their strength. They continued to rule in their own interest until the law was actually enforced. What makes this case interesting is that the Anti-Renters were advocating more democracy, not less. However, it is not simple democracy that conduces to individual development, but liberal democracy, which protects individuals from the encroachments of both the few and the many. Only a well-administered regime that values liberty as well as equality can serve as a suitable environment for individual growth. Thus the priority of liberalism to culture is twofold: security is a more fundamental good than cultural flourishing, and cultural development depends upon a delicate balance between self and other that can occur only in a democracy that defends individual liberty.[14]

The second category includes such phenomena as excessive material inequality, social exclusivity, and other forms of division that prevent people from viewing each other as equal members of a common association. Howells is most relevant on this score, as he brilliantly outlines how the excesses of capitalism undermine civic unity by degrading the poor and isolating the rich. In *A Hazard of New Fortunes,* Basil and Isabella March take carriage rides through Manhattan's lower-class neighborhoods, ostensibly to learn how the other half lives. However, the most they can do is sentimentalize the plight of the poor and marvel at the diversity of cultures. As members of the social elite, they are incapable of making a real connection with those below them—despite their interest in doing so. Howells notes that March is much better at observing and noting peculiarities of expression and behavior than at discovering "what these poor people were thinking, hoping, fearing, enjoying, suffering."[15] He has lived a life so distant from theirs that his attempts at bridging the gap are doomed to fail. Unfortunately, March is one of only a few members of the social elite who even try to connect with the less fortunate. Charitable causes proliferate among the rich, Howells notes, but only because contributing to them assuages one's conscience without requiring much sacrifice. Charity without fellow feeling is, at best, simple condescension, which reinforces the division between social classes. At worst, the advantaged classes use charity as a tool for gaining higher social standing. Consider, for example, Mrs. Makely's outline of the proper characteristics of a lady in *A Traveler from Altruria:* "Of course

14. *CY* 181. See also Cooper, *The Redskins,* in *Works of J. Fenimore Cooper,* vol. 6.

15. *HNF* 159. For an insightful commentary that links *A Hazard of New Fortunes* to Howells's actions on behalf of the Haymarket anarchists, see Everett Carter, *Howells and the Age of Realism,* 179–85, 201–15.

she must have a certain training. She must have cultivated tastes; she must know about art, and literature, and music, and all those kind of things, and though it isn't necessary to go in for anything in particular, it won't hurt her to have a fad or two. The nicest kind of fad is charity; and people go in for that a great deal. I think sometimes they use it to work up with, and there are some who use religion in the same way; I think it's horrid; but it's perfectly safe; you can't accuse them of doing it."[16] Where charity is a fad, the needy may still receive aid, but for the wrong reasons. Giving money or volunteering time in order to improve one's social standing, à la Mrs. Makely, hardly generates a culture of equal respect.

Vast material inequality and the social exclusivity it begets impair our ability to view each other as worthy participants in a common life. In *A Traveler from Altruria,* Howells writes of wealthy Bostonians who dine and dance their way through summer at elegant resorts, oblivious to the poverty afflicting the surrounding countryside. Although social functions are free and open to those from other resorts, local residents are excluded from participation. At dances they stand outside the hall, looking in through the windows, "not so much enviously . . . as wistfully."[17] Howells's symbolism is clear: modern capitalism separates the Haves and Have Nots to such a degree that, although they are aware of each other's presence, they might as well talk to each other through panes of thick glass. Formal equality before the law is important, but it does little for democratic interaction without a corresponding culture of liberal equality. This is not an argument for abandoning the free market, for doing so would destroy the preconditions of individual development. However, if we are truly concerned about human flourishing under democracy, we must at least consider whether some constraints on the market would be acceptable, if greater democratic interaction and individual development would result.

We must also come to terms with the undesirable vestiges of past regimes, such as racism, sexism, and religious bigotry—all of which obstruct free and equal interaction. Democracy, though, breeds its own varieties of prejudice, as citizens compete with each other for recognition, employment, and other social goods. Nativism, working-class racism, and the elit-

16. William Dean Howells, *A Traveler from Altruria,* 103.
17. Ibid., 95.

ism of the wealthy and educated classes could all be seen as resulting from the democratic struggle for autonomy, as certain groups attempt to secure a more privileged place within society, vis-à-vis their rivals.[18] These sorts of prejudices are more difficult to eradicate, since they arise from the regime we wish to preserve. With luck, though, a vibrant public sphere will soften the edges of these attitudes, and liberal legislation will prevent the institutionalization of prejudice. Fortunately, many of the intolerant attitudes found within modern liberal democracy are relics of older systems of thought, and can be excised without harming the regime. With the nondemocratic forms of prejudice removed, and the democratic forms softened, we can better engage in the sort of common dialogue that calls forth our best qualities—both civic and human.

In sum, I argue that democratic interaction, characterized by the full and fair exchange of ideas, not only can provide us with standards of justice (Habermas, Rawls) and make us better citizens (Tocqueville, Bellah et al.), but it also can make us better *human beings*. In the context of freedom and equality—the cultural bases of liberal democracy—we become adept at explaining ourselves to others and learning from them in turn. More than any other regime, liberal democracy removes barriers to genuine interaction, by securing individual rights and eliminating any formal advantages one might enjoy because of birth or status. We are all equal participants in democratic life, a fact that engenders a truly democratic form of skepticism— one that turns inward as well as outward.

The result is an arena in which our initial conceptions of nature and mankind, gleaned from our struggle for autonomy, are affirmed or qualified in talking with others. Our arrogant materialism is softened and refined, as we come to recognize the narrowness of a life devoted merely to physical comfort—especially if our own comfort entails the destruction of nobility in nature and in others. We gradually come to see what is important in life and what is truly worth pursuing. Add to this the fact that we come to this realization by ourselves, without indoctrination, and we may

18. For unblinking treatment of these (and related) problems, see Timothy B. Powell, *Ruthless Democracy;* and Philip Fisher, *Hard Facts,* esp. 73.

conclude that among possible regimes, liberal democracy *best* conduces to individual flourishing.

This is a somewhat idealized account of democracy, to be sure. However, if we succeed in eliminating the barriers to democratic interaction outlined above and in the next chapter, we can approach this ideal. This is what Cooper, Twain, and Howells hoped for. We should strive for it as well.

Conclusion

LIBERAL DEMOCRACY brashly eliminates the supposed elevating influences of aristocracy, theocracy, clerisy, and other formal hierarchies. However, it more than makes up the deficit by supplying a number of elevating forces *indirectly*. Liberal democracy places people in an unmediated, strenuous relationship with their environment, and the resultant challenges call forth a wider range of excellences than hierarchical relationships do.

The problem is that in their struggle for autonomy, people tend to cultivate those virtues that best enhance control over their environment—thus the emphasis on frugality, industry, ingenuity, and the like. Were this the endpoint of democratic development, we would either have to reject liberal democracy, as the aesthetic critics do, or defend it as the lesser of two evils: that is, as being seriously defective but nonetheless choiceworthy. Which alternative we choose depends on our relative valuation of peace, prosperity, and justice on the one hand, and nobility of character on the other. Given the disadvantages of aristocracy and the dangers of excessive state power, I (like most Americans) would probably stick with democracy, and hope for the best. There would be something deeply demoralizing about having to sacrifice the sort of full excellence the critics extol, but the alternative is far more disagreeable.

However, democratic development does not end with practical virtue. As I demonstrated in Chapter 3, the democratic struggle with nature and necessity, because a difficult one, causes people to take great pride in their achievement of autonomy. We inwardly celebrate our victories, and exhibit arrogance toward the obstacles we have overcome (recall Billy Kirby and his chopped trees). Though hardly desirable in its own right, this arrogance implies a second, more laudable attitude: a grudging appreciation of our opponent's worth. We tend to be arrogant regarding those accomplishments in which we take pride. No adult, for example, will boast of defeating a child at chess. Unless the contest is a challenging one, with a significant possibility of our *losing*, we have no reason to feel self-satisfied. The actions we do take pride in (winning a close game, catching a big fish, raising a child, improving our community) are generally those that involve a substantial struggle and an uncertain outcome.

The opposing team, the trophy bass, the challenges of parenthood, even one's political rivals (provided they are not devious or willfully evil) come to have a greater significance precisely because they have put us to the test. It is because they were worthy opponents that we can be proud of our victories. The team we have defeated is no longer just a collection of people in uniforms, toward whom we have no particular aversion or attraction. They have become noble rivals who pushed us to excel—and, given different circumstances or greater luck, could have beaten us.

Implicit in our arrogance is a recognition of the nobility of the people or things against which we have struggled. The world becomes, in our view, more than something to master. Our arrogant materialism provides the groundwork and motivating force for a more enlightened appreciation of the world and its inhabitants. In fact, the appreciation we feel is deeper and broader than what aristocrats feel, since it pervades almost every aspect of our lives.

Incidentally, Charles Dickens misses this in his portrayal of Josiah Bounderby, a self-made man who continually boasts of his rise from poverty. Dickens takes the easy path in *Hard Times* by revealing Bounderby as a fraud. The book would have been far more interesting had he allowed Bounderby to be a genuine, truthful character. If we were to examine Bounderby's pride more closely (and free it from the distortions of caricature), we would likely find it deriving from a real appreciation of the challenges he faced as a child, and a desire to gain recognition for his achievements. Bounderby has romanticized his own struggle for autonomy, the conditions of his poverty, and the meaning of his success, which demonstrates that there is something in him—and others like him—that Dickens fails to notice. There *is* something noble about Bounderby's rise from the gutter, though it is hidden by the arrogant materialism Dickens ridicules. Like most successful people, Bounderby is capable of further development—and in fact contains within himself the basic sentiments necessary to drive such development. Compared to Dickens, Howells is far more attentive to the complexities of the self-made person's motivations in his analysis of Silas Lapham and Jacob Dryfoos.

Were we to stop here, we would still have failed to provide an adequate answer to the critics. Our struggle for autonomy may give us a deeper appreciation of the world, but our arrogant materialism still overshadows that appreciation. Unless we can find a way to encourage the desirable but underlying sentiments, while keeping our dominant materialist impulses in check, our justification of liberal democracy will be mere talk about potentialities.

Fortunately, healthy liberal democracy provides a remedy for the problem of narrowly developed people: the public sphere. Constructed on the basis of equality and liberty, the democratic public sphere compels us to explain ourselves to others, listen to responses with respect, and gradually assimilate new ideas with our existing ones. Our hard edges become softened, our nobler sentiments become confirmed, and we slowly become better developed as a whole. We may not all become spectacularly well developed (this is an impossible dream), but most people will be improved by this process of liberation, struggle, and refinement.

Have I fully answered the critics? Probably not. It would be impossible to satisfy all of them completely, given their own differences of opinion. What unites them, however, is a conviction that under conditions of equal liberty, citizens will invariably tend toward mediocrity, conformity, and petty materialism. Granting negative liberty to people will simply give them greater opportunity for choosing poorly. Given this scenario, would it not be better to give additional political power to those who can make good use of liberty, and entrust everyone else to their care and guidance?

I believe I have made a strong case against this general argument. Though the sort of individual development possible within liberal democracy may be at odds with some of the critics' ideals, it is nonetheless vastly preferable to the petty materialism the critics rightly despise. It does not sacrifice nobility, and it has the added advantage of being democratic. Nearly all democratic citizens are exposed to the indirect elevating effects that equal liberty creates, and subsequently can undergo significant amounts of development. The gain to humanity of having a democratic ideal of individual development far outweighs any sacrifice of spectacular excellence we might have to make. So even if the critics will not be fully satisfied, chances are they will be mollified. Democracy, if properly understood and properly ordered, is hardly the threat to world civilization the critics make it out to be. In addition, it is not clear that this conception of individual development precludes the cultivation of genius. Genius tends to spring up without regard for the form of political institutions, and can flourish without aristocratic patronage.

At the same time, my argument provides the beginnings of a response to those critics on the Left who would question my reluctance to advocate more-revolutionary action. After all, if conditions of liberty and equality prompt fuller individual development, why not eliminate all the factors that distort one's character, such as private property and the capitalist relationship to labor? My initial reply is that liberal democracy is fertile enough ground for individual development, and we can achieve a reasonably high level of culture without resorting to revolution. When one considers the tangible and intangible costs of communist revolution—costs that make communism not only difficult to achieve but perhaps even undesirable as an end—it is comforting to know that a more moderate regime can provide much of the same type of development that Marx envisioned in his utopia. Liberal democrats will probably never transform themselves completely into species beings, but they are capable of transcending and likely will transcend the narrowness of soul that both Marx and the aesthetic critics despised.

A further concern with communist revolution is that Marx is rather ambiguous about what motivates communists to engage in meaningful activities. To his credit, Marx points out that it is in our nature—our genuine nature—to seek to produce beautiful things, but he neither fully appreciates how our creative spirit depends on a close engagement with the world around us nor satisfactorily explains how the structure of communism encourages this interaction. By removing the element of individualist struggle from the human experience, he eliminates the most powerful incentive toward developing one's faculties. Relying on the remaining incentive—

our spontaneous creative impulses—seems overly optimistic in the face of the aesthetic critique. Even the aristocratic critics realize the necessity of prodding people to do more than follow their momentary whims (recall James Fitzjames Stephen's quip about the marsh water not running to the sea). Given the violence and injustice necessary to achieve the communist ideal, and the uncertainty of individual development within communist society, there is little reason to abandon liberal democracy for it.[1]

Individual Development and State Action

The question of "proper" ordering leads us to consider the role of government in encouraging citizens' development. At this point, it is crucial to emphasize that my argument is not fundamentally a libertarian one, though at times it appears to be. Robert Nozick's contention that "[t]he minimal state is the most extensive state that can be justified"[2] is incompatible with democratic development, for a substantial amount of state action is necessary to preserve the conditions that indirectly promote development. In this section, I sketch out how a concern for both liberal democracy and individual development might shape one's approach to public policy.

First, it is necessary to discuss the priority that individual development should have relative to other social values, such as justice, peace, and prosperity. In a sense, individual development is more important than these other ends, since it exposes us to truths that have significance beyond the realm of human interaction. However, as a concern of political action, individual development should generally be subordinated to other fundamental social concerns. Without justice, peace, and a reasonable amount of prosperity, individual development diminishes in importance. It also becomes less *possible* under these chaotic conditions, thus making justice a more fundamental good in two senses.

It is impossible, though, to prescribe a universal principle for ordering these goods. Much depends on the particular needs and values of concrete communities. There are likely to be situations where individual develop-

1. *The German Ideology*, in *Karl Marx: Selected Writings*.
2. Robert Nozick, *Anarchy, State, and Utopia*, 149.

ment deserves political priority over prosperity, and there may even be times (however rare) when it should take precedence over peace and justice. When such circumstances present themselves, the decision to prioritize individual development should undergo strict scrutiny.

A more interesting possibility is that by giving greater attention to what promotes and hinders individual development, we might come to modify our conceptions of injustice and injury. If a given action does no physical harm to my life or my property, yet works to stifle my development as a full human being, is it nevertheless just? Does my status as a developing human give me an additional claim vis-à-vis state and society, which would enjoy the same validity as other protestations of harm?[3]

It is difficult to make detailed policy recommendations based on this study, since it deals with only one of several essential concerns of legislators. What I *can* outline, however, is a set of recommendations and justifications that can be balanced against other political values. To this end, I shall briefly examine three possible ways in which a liberal democratic government can encourage individual development: establishing conditions of equal liberty, ensuring that autonomy is possible through individual effort, and creating the foundations for a vibrant public sphere.

Establishing Equal Liberty

This is the most fundamental contribution that liberal democratic government can make to the cause of individual development. Unless people feel equally free and worthy, individual development will occur only within a small minority of the population. Achieving this requires governmental action in several areas. First, a system of equal basic rights and liberties must be established and sustained, consistent with the notion that all people deserve the opportunity to direct their own lives, provided they harm no one in the process. As Twain's satirical depiction of Camelot demonstrates, living under hierarchical forms of government stifles our sense of self-importance and prevents us from thinking independently. Unless we are allowed to view the world without the mediation of a temporal authority (or a spiritual authority with temporal powers, like the Church of

---

3. Mill gestures this direction in *On Liberty,* in his discussion of the majority's unjust suppression of individuality.

Arthurian Britain), and unless we can make our own judgments, individual development will be unlikely.

The content of these provisions is open to some debate, but they would probably overlap with the rights contained in the U.S. Constitution (freedom of expression and religion, freedom from unreasonable searches and seizures, equality before the law, and so forth). Nor does it matter much, for our purposes, which particular liberal justifications (Rawlsian, Kantian, utilitarian, and so forth) are offered for the basic rights. As long as they are securely protected, they will provide an adequate foundation for individual development.

Second, government should work to ensure that citizens possess adequate resources for actively enjoying their rights. Although there is great disagreement about what constitutes sufficient substantive equality, it is unlikely that mere formal equality is enough to give people the sense of empowered dignity that makes further development possible. On the other hand, excessive welfare statism limits freedom of action and stifles the spirit of independence—values that are equally essential to development. As a result, legislators should seek to ensure a level of subsistence that makes the exercise of liberty a real possibility for all, without engendering new forms of dependence.

Third, government should combat the lingering, mind-numbing effects of obsolete regimes, like those Cooper, Twain, and Howells describe in Chapter 2. How is it to accomplish this without transgressing traditional liberal principles? Would not actions regulating such effects undermine free expression? In many cases, yes. Liberalism implies a reluctance to restrict even offensive speech, so long as it causes or incites no tangible physical harm. On liberal principles, even Ku Klux Klan members should be allowed to stage peaceful public rallies. Beyond preventing physical harm to its citizens, a liberal government can only make sure that the members of offensive organizations have not been coerced into joining. These governmental activities may set boundaries for offensive or antidemocratic action, but they do little against the central effects of peaceful demonstrations of hate and racism.

Fortunately, although direct governmental action in these cases would be illiberal, there are subtler, more indirect methods for ensuring a favorable environment for individual development. Primary among these is public education, the goal of which should be to create independent, critically thinking beings. After all, the surest way to prevent people from rejecting democracy and its potential for individual development is to get them to think for themselves. Otherwise, they will either fall prey to the Jason Newcomes of the world, who care nothing for democracy and equal liberty except insofar as they advance their own interests, or simply conform to prevalent standards of value, as Silas Lapham did. However, make people independent in spirit as well as law, and tyranny—whether the old-fashioned hierarchical kind or the modern majoritarian kind—will cease to be a threat. Education can accomplish this within the framework of liberalism, by encouraging children to think originally and to inquire into the reasons behind others' arguments.

This is not a completely neutral attitude toward education, since it prioritizes independent reasoning over conformity to received truth. Yet liberalism itself is not strictly neutral with respect to competing ends; it is just *more* neutral than other possible regimes.[4] Likewise, liberal education is more neutral than, for example, the ideal-based public education that Matthew Arnold advocates. As such, it serves as a crucial sustaining force behind equal liberty.

Ensuring Autonomy

The second general category of state action on behalf of individual development concerns the preservation of the unique balance between autonomy and necessity that brings out people's best qualities. In Chapter 3, I discussed how democracy makes it possible for people to achieve a degree of autonomy over their lives, but only through a constant struggle with nature and other humans. Democrats are neither subordinate nor superior to their neighbors, which leads to anxiety and competition. No one will look out for us if we fail to provide for ourselves. Although we have the right to participate in communal rule, we do not enjoy the comfortable subsistence of aristocrats. We must work for what we enjoy, a fact that causes us to develop a wide range of practical virtues. Yet, this is only possible if workplace and political conditions enable a sort of difficult autonomy.

4. For liberal arguments rejecting the idea of neutrality, see William Galston, *Liberal Purposes;* and Stephen Macedo, *Liberal Virtues.*

The ideal workplace environment for individual development is, generally speaking, one in which workers share in decision making and enjoy a significant amount of responsibility.[5] It is not necessary that they be self-employed, as long as they are not coerced into working and are treated as valuable associates in a common venture. Even disagreeable jobs, like trash collecting, are not inconsistent with individual development, as long as workers actually participate in company policy making.[6] When people retain a significant degree of control over their destinies as workers, they come to see greater meaning in the world. In his "Address to the Wisconsin State Agricultural Society," Abraham Lincoln argued that free-soil farmers find in agriculture "an exhaustless source of profitable enjoyment." "Every blade of grass," he continued, "is a study; and to produce two, where there was but one, is both a profit and a pleasure." Even crop diseases, hogs, and fences become endowed with greater significance when viewed by a farmer who labors for himself. The same is true, though sometimes to a lesser degree, of all work done with an independent spirit (even if for wages).[7]

The flip side is that work should not be too easy. Those who enjoy decision-making power without having to work for that privilege (having inherited their jobs or received them as favors) will tend to be not only poor managers, but unevenly developed individuals. For them, autonomy came too easily, much as it does for aristocrats. Nepotism may have its advantages (it may even be quite efficient at times), but it does not conduce well to individual development.

To the extent that we would like people to develop their individual potentials, we should seek to ensure that work is both *challenging* and *rewarding:* challenging so that employees' best traits are brought out, and rewarding so that they feel significant. It is that sense of contributing some-

5. See, for example, David Michael Smith, "Workplace Democracy at College of the Mainland," 257–62. For a thoughtful consideration of the obstacles and challenges to workplace democratization, see Linda Markowitz, "Employee Participation at the Workplace," 89–103.

6. See Walzer's discussion of the Sunset Scavenger Company of San Francisco in *Spheres of Justice.*

7. Lincoln, "Address to the Wisconsin State Agricultural Society," in *Selected Speeches and Writings,* 236. Of course, certain forms of voluntary labor (sharecropping, ditchdigging) will tend to have a smaller positive effect on individual development.

thing valuable that fosters the self-respect necessary for fuller development and the pride that impels it onward.

What role can government play in maintaining this balance between challenge and autonomy in the workplace? Within the confines of liberalism, not much can be done directly—other than ensuring that the criterion of consent is satisfied (that is, not allowing forced labor). However, even limited government, as a player in the free marketplace, possesses a wealth of instruments for shaping society indirectly. In the realm of government contracts, for example, private companies must generally meet a number of criteria before being hired to provide goods or services. Some of these criteria are oriented around the demands of justice (Does Company X discriminate in hiring?), while others concern efficiency (How cheap and reliable are X's goods?). It seems both possible and reasonable to insert additional criteria that would focus on a company's corporate culture. Are conditions at X such that employees are able to work as thinking human beings, not mere automatons? Do the owners include workers in decision-making processes? These variables may be difficult to measure, but much can be accomplished simply by requiring bidders to explain their company's efforts to increase worker autonomy, and making their claims subject to verification.

All things being equal, it would be perfectly consistent with liberal democratic principles for government to give priority to companies providing working conditions favorable to individual development over companies that do not. Such concerns, though generally subordinate to questions of justice, might at times outweigh concerns of efficiency. A company that turns in a lower bid, but has a poor record of treating its employees with respect, should not automatically get the nod—especially if the bids are relatively similar. Though it would be unjust to require all companies to adopt these more stringent standards, it is less troublesome to introduce them into the government's contracting procedure. Even liberal government cannot be oblivious to the state of its citizens' character, and a company that stifles citizens' individuality should not receive the same priority as one that actively works to improve its employees' workplace experience.

Individual development can also be enhanced by empowering people as citizens. Political participation ought to be encouraged, not just for the civic-mindedness it fosters, but for the more general effects it has on people's outlook. When we engage in collective action for some political end, we place ourselves in a situation where we have the opportunity to change our community for the better (that is, to assert our autonomy as citizens), but only through a more-or-less difficult ordeal. This combination of possibilities and obstacles brings out our civic and practical virtues, thereby beginning the process of individual development.

Ideally, political authority should be concentrated in states and localities, where the actions of citizens can have a direct and tangible effect on public policy. When government is distant and unresponsive, people become quiescent and tend to lack the self-confidence necessary for development in other areas. Of course, a variety of other concerns, such as national defense and the desire for consistent standards of justice, often justify greater nationalization of political authority. However, legislators must realize that centralization can have a detrimental effect not only on civic virtue, but on individual development as a whole. Take power (or potential power) out of the people's hands, and you unbalance the relationship between opportunity and obstacle, making the achievement of real autonomy nearly impossible for most people.

The need for centralization will outweigh this concern at certain points in time (during war, for example), but we should at least be aware of the full costs of centralization. We should evaluate each plan for increased centralization not only on whether it will provide greater security, more consistent justice, or a larger GNP, but also on whether it creates conditions favorable to a vibrant civic culture—or, more broadly, whether it makes it more possible for people to attain a degree of mastery over their environment. Achieving a reasonable amount of autonomy under conditions of equal liberty is difficult enough, given the nature of the competition, without the state artificially reducing the chances of success. To the extent that a community takes individual development seriously, the dominant political bias should be in favor of decentralization. Claims for greater centralization should undergo close scrutiny, given centralization's potential for stifling individual development—civic or otherwise.

More generally, government should work to ensure that all citizens can achieve a fair amount of control over the course of their lives. This involves making it possible for citizens not only to exercise their formal rights effectively (as argued above), but to achieve a degree of mastery over material necessity. Thus, there is a dual argument for a guaranteed minimum level of subsistence. Where this level is pegged at any given time is open to legislative debate, but it should be high enough to prevent people from utterly degrading themselves, but low enough so that the achievement of autonomy is still difficult. It should not be so high, for example, as to remove the spur to industry among able-bodied people, by making work unnecessary.

Liberal government should do what it can, consistent with its principles, to preserve the element of struggle in the democratic experience. The "pursuit of happiness" should not be construed simply as a formal right—and thus impossible for most people to achieve—nor should the state attempt to provide its citizens with full happiness. It is the *pursuit* that is key: the active striving for a goal, with a likely but uncertain chance of success. Government should provide what is necessary to make this pursuit possible (preservation of property rights, a welfare safety net, and so forth), but it should leave the actual pursuit to individuals. This is both consistent with liberalism and conducive to individual development.

The debate over welfare tends to run to extremes. Liberals justify expansive welfare programs as compensating for structural forms of inequality, arguing that it is not the fault of the poor for being poor. In their eyes, poverty results from factors beyond the individual's control, such as racism or the vagaries of the business cycle. As members of the same community, they argue, we have a duty to provide for the poor, not judge them. Conservatives take the opposite tack, emphasizing the ways in which the poor have themselves to blame for their poverty. Handouts simply encourage laziness, they argue. As noted in Chapter 3, civic republicans tend to take a middle course, calling for a conception of welfare centered on making self-government a real possibility. My argument operates along similar lines, advocating a level of government provision sufficient to ensure that the individual's struggle for autonomy is a fair fight, but no more. Providing too little or too much risks degrading people, for they will either despair of success or take it for granted. Neither attitude is conducive to individual development.

Preserving the Public Sphere

The democratic public sphere's positive effects on individual development are clear, but it is also evident that establishing and maintaining a vibrant public sphere is difficult work—especially when government has virtually no power to compel people to associate with each other. How are we to ensure that democratic interaction takes place?

The first step is to guarantee that when people *do* interact, they do so within a context of freedom and equality. Of course, no actual discussion will ever fulfill the conditions of Habermas's ideal speech situation, but government can prevent certain dangerous inequalities from creeping in. Preserving a person's right to exit a conversation is one example, as is preventing discussion from devolving into violence. These typical liberal provisions may not do much directly to encourage interaction, but by making interaction safer and more equal, they increase the chances that people will participate.

Aside from these obvious liberal actions, government can work to provide and preserve public spaces, where people of all classes have no choice but to encounter each other. Historically, public parks, playgrounds, and beaches have helped accomplish this end, as have centrally located public buildings. City planners should use their zoning powers not just to attract businesses or protect wealthy neighborhoods, but (insofar as possible) to structure residential and commercial areas in ways that funnel people of different backgrounds into common areas. The town green at the center of many American communities, surrounded by important public, commercial, and residential buildings, is a classic—but by no means the only—example. The so-called New Urbanists, in adapting the insights of traditional mixed-use city planning to the twenty-first century, share a similar concern for diverse public interaction.[8] Of course, no one will frequent public spaces if they are unsafe; therefore, communities should also commit to making their public spaces their least dangerous areas.

I am not suggesting that encouraging cross-class interaction should be the primary goal of city government, or that any of this can be accomplished without expense. However, the long-range good associated with safe, accessible public spaces would seem to justify considerable expenditure. As with all reforms, the first step is articulating a clear vision; if peo-

8. See, for example, Congress of the New Urbanism, *Charter of the New Urbanism;* Jay Wickersham, "Jane Jacobs's Critique of Zoning: From *Euclid* to Portland and Beyond"; Philip Bess, "Design Matters"; and Catesby Leigh, "It Takes a (Well-Planned) Village."

ple are convinced of the plan's value, vis-à-vis other concerns, they will be likely to finance it.

By far the most important arena in which liberal democracy can advance the cause of individual development is in public education. The public educational system brings together children of all races and backgrounds, compels them to be in the same room with each other, and makes it impossible for them *not* to interact with each other—whether in the classroom, at lunch, or during recess. As Howells demonstrates in *A Traveler from Altruria,* members of the same social class tend to interact excessively with each other, while remaining aloof from members of other classes. Public education removes the glass walls of class, race, and ethnicity, thereby exposing children to different viewpoints and giving them experience in interacting with people who are not like them. Extracurricular activities only enhance this effect, by cohering diverse students into a group or team devoted to a common interest. In this context, the lifelong democratic process of expressing, defending, and modifying one's opinions in the company of others begins vigorously. Moreover, as the most important of public spaces, schools should be made the safest places in the city.

Since my argument asserts that individual development depends on exposure to viewpoints at odds with one's own, it tends to undermine the case for private elementary and secondary schools. Such schools, available only to those whose parents can afford the tuition, strip away an entire segment of students from the public schools. This causes a severe decrease in the number and type of different outlooks students are exposed to, in both public *and* private schools. In addition, the upper-class flight to private schools erodes community support for public schools, and removes from the equation many parents who would otherwise be active in shaping school policy. There is something democratically important about making a person who drives a Mercedes wait in the same line at the post office as the driver of a second-hand Pinto. The same is true of schools. Give some people an exemption, and those who remain will resent both the privileged few and the system that granted their privileges. This resentment will destroy any chances for the interclass dialogue and understanding necessary for individual development.

Matthew Arnold advocated using public schools as a medium for transmitting society's highest ideals. Yet imposing communal norms in this manner is in considerable tension with liberalism, which highly values individual choice. A better approach would be to think of education as a means of broadening students' outlook, of exposing them to new knowledge and viewpoints—not simply educating them toward one ideal of citizenship or human development. Naturally, a curriculum is limited in what it can accomplish, but it is not necessary to expose students to *everything*.[9] As long as in the course of their education students are confronted with ideas that challenge their beliefs, they will acquire the intellectual skills that, when combined with habits of democratic interaction, will enable them to rise above petty forms of materialism.

Democratic Theory and the Novel

Before concluding, I would like to say a few words about using novels to understand politics. Though the politics and literature movement is gaining momentum, incorporating literary analysis into political theory still raises a number of methodological issues. In the Introduction, I discussed some of the advantages of using novels; in this section I will discuss two further aspects of the relationship between literature and political theory: first, how to evaluate arguments that draw upon literary examples, and second, whether narrative fiction as a mode of expression is inherently biased.

Concerning the first, how ought one judge the argument of this book? How can a theoretical argument be legitimate if it rests upon fictional examples? Could one not find or construct whatever examples one likes, in order to justify a preconceived argument? To a point, these objections are well founded. It is difficult to give fiction the same evidentiary status as deductive proofs or observations of actual behavior. However, there is a standard that can be used to determine whether a fictional example can be relied upon: the test of plausibility. In other words, is the novelist's depiction of character and plot reasonably true to life?

One advantage of novels is that they are intended to resonate with their readers; thus, characters tend to represent types or classes of people, not dis-

---

9. Amy Gutmann notes that while a solid democratic education will include cosmopolitan foci, the central emphasis should remain on the students' own history and culture. Gutmann, *Democratic Education*, 316.

crete individuals. For instance, we come to identify with Huckleberry Finn because we recognize certain aspects of his character as also residing in us, or in humans in general. Sometimes we do not identify personally with a character, but we are familiar with people similar to him or her. Jacob Dryfoos or Jason Newcome might be examples of this type. Even caricatures or unrealistic plots can convey something meaningful about the human condition—as any reader of Twain knows. The crucial thing to determine is whether a given novel or illustration actually conveys such truth. Is Silas Lapham an adequate representation of the typical self-made man? Does Hank Morgan embody the chief traits of a Yankee democrat? Given the setting and plot of the novel, do the characters act in a plausible fashion? If so, then that novel is a reliable source for political insight. In general, quality novels are at least as reliable as empirical observation—and often more so, since in crafting characters who are representative of actual types of people, novelists have already begun the process of generalizing that is central to political theory.

When a given illustration seems implausible, it is necessary to determine whether the political theorist is at fault for overinterpreting or misapplying the novel, or whether the novelist has constructed a character or plot that bears little resemblance to reality. In either case, it is appropriate to offer the theorist alternate interpretations of the novel in question or to provide literary or empirical examples that challenge the argument of the novel itself. However, just because a literary example is proven implausible does not necessarily prove false the overarching theoretical argument. It just means that the theory is deprived of certain evidentiary underpinnings. A greater problem arises when a misinterpreted literary example would, if interpreted more accurately, provide evidence contrary to the overall theoretical argument. Whereas in the former case, the argument's truth is not questioned, in the latter the argument itself faces a direct challenge. I hope my argument will survive both types of criticism.

I originally justified my use of literature in terms of its ability to provide a more complex account of democratic life than traditional methods of political discourse. However, I wish to add a caveat, especially since using literature in political theory has become increasingly popular. Although it is true that political theorists—in particular democratic theorists—have historically tended to downplay the importance of particularity and difference in their search for the universal or general, reliance upon literature can lead to the opposite problem: excessive emphasis on the particular. Whereas political theorists focus on the characteristics all people (or all people in a community) share, novelists concern themselves with detailed descriptions of identifiable individuals in concrete, unique situations. The governing bias of theoretical discourses is toward abstraction and simplicity, that of novels toward particularity and complexity. The dangers of the former have prompted theorists to embrace literature, but the dangers of the latter make it imperative that we use literature judiciously.

The novel has great value in demonstrating how general laws fail to account for the variety of conditions under which individuals actually live. It is best suited to showing how each person's case is distinct from all others, and how categorization inevitably causes injustice. Literature exposes the falsehood inherent in categories and reminds us that our commitment to equality requires us to ignore people's obvious differences in strength, beauty, and intelligence. As a mode of political inquiry, literature pulls us toward a conception of justice that emphasizes giving people their due, where each person's due is unique.

This aspect of literary thought, when untempered by the traditional theoretical emphasis on universality, is subversive of democracy. Democracy, after all, rests on the notion that all people deserve equal respect and equal treatment before the law. Focusing too much on differences, without emphasizing similarities, leads to aristocratic, not democratic conclusions. I do not mean to suggest that we consciously reject truth when we shy away from the literary emphasis on particularity. On the contrary: we ought to reject both the purely abstract and the purely particularist modes of thought, and search for a reasonable synthesis.

I have hinted at two ways in which this may be accomplished. First, we must realize that most novels, though containing seemingly particular characters and plotlines, in fact exhibit a fair degree of generalization. This is necessary to make the novel attractive to readers (so they can find something to identify with) and to give it intellectual significance (that is, to capture something important about the human condition—not just *this* human's condition). Second, following Maureen Whitebrook's suggestion, we should think of novels as occupying a mediating role between political theory and political practice. Novels, when done well, partake of both the universal and particular aspects of democratic life, and are good tests of abstract arguments before they are actually embodied in law. Put more strongly, it is only by thinking as storytellers that we can make sense of our theoretical speculations; unless we can explain our theories through story or analogy, we do not fully understand them—or know how to apply them wisely. Though novels can exhibit a particularist bias when considered on their own, when read as part of a larger theoretical project they can provide valuable insight and substance. They help make theory practical—the precondition for using theory to elevate political practice.

Though I have reached the end of this work, it is important to note that it is only a preliminary investigation into the relationship between liberal democracy and individual development. One could write volumes more about liberal democracy and its effects; the nature of individual development; and the particular views of Cooper, Twain, Howells, and the aesthetic critics. In the interest of clarity and brevity, I have exhausted none of these topics.

My purpose has been to offer a defense of liberal democracy that takes seriously the value of individual development. Although in the end the likelihood of cultivating well-developed citizens within liberal democracy may not be tremendously high, it is at least greater than the critics make it out to be, owing to subtle but powerful mechanisms at work beneath the surface of liberal democracy. When appropriate political reforms are enacted, the effects of these mechanisms will be even more evident.

Is liberal democracy a good model for the future? Yes, but not precisely for the reasons typically offered. Justice, peace, and prosperity are certainly valuable social goods, and liberal democracy effectively secures them. However, there is more to human existence than living fairly and comfortably. The idea that the inactive, quiescent life is somehow contrary to what it means to be human drives the republican argument for civic virtue, and a similar concern underlies my argument. Unless people are able to realize their unique capacities, justice and comfort lose some of their significance. Fortunately, liberal democracy is not inimical to individual development, but subtly prods it along. For this reason liberal democracy, despite its flaws, is in fact a very good model for the future.

Bibliography

Arendt, Hannah. *The Human Condition.* Chicago: University of Chicago Press, 1958.

Aristotle. *The Politics.* Ed. Stephen Everson. Trans. Benjamin Jowett. Cambridge: Cambridge University Press, 1996.

Arnold, Matthew. *Civilization in the United States.* Freeport, NY: Books for Libraries Press, 1972.

———. *Selected Prose.* Ed. P. J. Keating. New York: Penguin, 1970.

Baetzhold, Howard. *Mark Twain and John Bull.* Bloomington: Indiana University Press, 1970.

Barba, Preston A. "Cooper in Germany." *German American Annals* 12, no. 1 (1914): 3–60.

Barber, Benjamin R. *Jihad vs. McWorld.* New York: Ballantine Books, 1996.

———. *Strong Democracy.* Berkeley: University of California Press, 1984.

Bellah, Robert, et al. *Habits of the Heart.* Berkeley: University of California Press, 1985.

Benhabib, Seyla, ed. *Democracy and Difference.* Princeton: Princeton University Press, 1996.

Bercovitch, Sacvan, and Myra Jehlen, eds. *Ideologoy and Classic American Literature.* Cambridge: Cambridge University Press, 1987.

Berlin, Isaiah. *Four Essays on Liberty.* Oxford: Oxford University Press, 1969.

Bess, Philip. "Design Matters." *Christian Century* 120, no. 8 (April 19, 2003): 20–23.

Blau, Joseph L., ed. *Social Theories of Jacksonian Democracy.* New York: The Liberal Arts Press, 1954.

Block, James E. *A Nation of Agents.* Cambridge: Harvard University Press, 2002.

Bloom, Harold, ed. *Mark Twain's Adventures of Huckleberry Finn.* New York: Chelsea House Publishers, 1986.

Bohlmann, Otto. *Yeats and Nietzsche.* Totowa, NJ: Barnes & Noble Books, 1982.

Booth, Wayne C. *The Rhetoric of Fiction.* Chicago: University of Chicago Press, 1983.

Brooks, Van Wyck. *Howells: His Life and World.* New York: E. P. Dutton, 1959.

Buchanan, Patrick J. *The Great Betrayal.* Boston: Little, Brown, 1998.

Budd, Louis. *Mark Twain: Social Philosopher.* Bloomington: Indiana University Press, 1962.

Buell, Lawrence. *The Environmental Imagination.* Cambridge: Harvard University Press, 1995.

Carlyle, Thomas. *Latter-Day Pamphlets.* Essay Index Reprint Series. Hallandale, FL: New World Book Manufacturing, 1972.

————. *Past and Present.* London: Everyman, 1915.

Carter, Everett. *Howells and the Age of Realism.* New York: J. B. Lippincott, 1954.

Cawelti, John. *Apostles of the Self-Made Man.* Chicago: University of Chicago Press, 1965.

Congress of the New Urbanism. *Charter of the New Urbanism.* [n.d.] http://www.cnu.org/aboutcnu.

Cooper, James Fenimore. *The American Democrat.* Indianapolis: Liberty Fund, 1959.

————. *Works of J. Fenimore Cooper.* 10 vols. New York: P. F. Collier, 1892.

Cuddy, Lois A., and David H. Hirsch, eds. *Critical Essays on T. S. Eliot's "The Waste Land."* Boston: G. K. Hall, 1991.

Dickens, Charles. *American Notes for General Circulation.* New York: Penguin, 1985.

————. *Hard Times.* New York: New American Library, 1961.

Dimock, Wai Chee. *Residues of Justice.* Berkeley: University of California Press, 1996.

Eliot, T. S. *The Complete Poems and Plays: 1909–1950.* New York: Harcourt, Brace, 1958.

————. *The Idea of a Christian Society.* New York: Harcourt, Brace, 1940.

Ellison, Ralph. *Invisible Man.* New York: Random House, 1995.

Emerson, Ralph Waldo. *Essays and Lectures.* New York: Library of America, 1983.

————. *Representative Men.* Cambridge: Harvard University Press, 1996.

————. *Selected Essays.* Ed. Larzer Ziff. New York: Penguin, 1982.

Espada, Martín. "Coca-Cola and Coco Frío." http://www.martinespada.net/cocacola.htm.

Filmer, Robert. *Patriarcha and Other Writings.* Ed. Johann P. Sommerville. Cambridge: Cambridge University Press, 1991.

Fisher, Philip. *Hard Facts.* New York: Oxford University Press, 1987.

Foucault, Michel. *Discipline and Punish.* Trans. Alan Sheridan. New York: Vintage Books, 1977.

Friedman, Thomas. *The Lexus and the Olive Tree.* New York: Anchor Books, 2000.

Fukuyama, Francis. *The End of History and the Last Man.* New York: HarperCollins, 1992.

Galston, William. *Liberal Purposes*. Cambridge: Cambridge University Press, 1991.

Gilman, Charlotte Perkins. *Herland*. New York: Pantheon, 1979.

———. *The Yellow Wall-Paper and Other Writings*. New York: The Modern Library, 2000.

Gutmann, Amy. *Democratic Education*. Princeton: Princeton University Press, 1987.

Habermas, Jürgen. *Between Facts and Norms*. Trans. William Rehg. Cambridge: MIT Press, 1996.

Hayek, Friedrich. *The Constitution of Liberty*. Chicago: University of Chicago Press, 1960.

Herder, Johann Gottfried von. *J. G. Herder on Social and Political Culture*. Ed. F. M. Barnard. Cambridge: Cambridge University Press, 1969.

Hobbes, Thomas. *Leviathan*. Ed. C. B. Macpherson. New York: Penguin, 1968.

Hoffman, Andrew. *Twain's Heroes, Twain's Worlds*. Philadelphia: University of Pennsylvania Press, 1988.

Horton, John, and Andrea T. Baumeister, eds. *Literature and the Political Imagination*. London: Routledge, 1996.

House, Kay Seymour. *Cooper's Americans*. Columbus: Ohio State University Press, 1965.

Howe, Daniel Walker. *Making the American Self*. Cambridge: Harvard University Press, 1997.

Howe, Irving. *Politics and the Novel*. Chicago: Ivan R. Dee, 1987.

Howells, William Dean. "Editor's Study." *Harper's New Monthly Magazine* 80, no. 476 (January 1890): 318–21.

———. *A Hazard of New Fortunes*. New York: Penguin Books, 1965.

———. *The Rise of Silas Lapham*. New York: Penguin Books, 1971.

———. *A Traveler from Altruria*. New York: Harper and Brothers, 1894.

Hughes, Langston. "The Negro Artist and the Racial Mountain." *The Nation*. June 23, 1926.

Humboldt, Wilhelm von. *The Limits of State Action*. Ed. J. W. Burrow. Indianapolis: Liberty Fund, 1969.

Huntington, Samuel. *The Clash of Civilizations and the Remaking of World Order*. New York: Simon and Schuster, 1998.

Jefferson, Thomas. *The Portable Thomas Jefferson*. Ed. Merrill D. Peterson. New York: Penguin, 1965.

Johnson, James. "Comment" on "Public Sphere, Postmodernism and Polemic." *American Political Science Review* 88, no. 2 (1994): 427–30.

Jones, Howard Mumford. *Jeffersonianism and the American Novel*. New York: Teachers College Press, 1966.

Kahan, Alan S. *Aristocratic Liberalism*. New York: Oxford University Press, 1992.

Kant, Immanuel. *Grounding for the Metaphysics of Morals.* Trans. James W. Elling-
ton. Indianapolis: Hackett, 1981.

————. *The Metaphysics of Morals.* Ed. Mary Gregor. Cambridge: Cambridge
University Press, 1996.

————. *Kant: Political Writings.* Ed. Hans Reiss. Trans. H. B. Nisbet. Cambridge:
Cambridge University Press, 1991.

————. *Kant: Selections.* Ed. Lewis White Beck. Englewood Cliffs, NJ: Prentice
Hall, 1988.

Kateb, George. *Emerson and Self-Reliance.* Thousand Oaks: Sage, 1995.

————. *The Inner Ocean.* Ithaca, NY: Cornell University Press, 1992.

Konvitz, Milton R., and Stephen E. Whicher, eds. *Emerson: A Collection of Critical Essays.* Englewood Cliffs, NJ: Prentice Hall, 1962.

Krause, Sydney J. *Mark Twain as Critic.* Baltimore: Johns Hopkins University
Press, 1967.

Lara, Maria Pia. *Moral Textures.* Los Angeles: University of California Press, 1998.

Lawrence, D. H. *Studies in Classic American Literature.* New York: Penguin, 1961.

Leigh, Catesby. "It Takes a (Well-Planned) Village." *National Review* 55, no. 13
(July 14, 2003): 34–37.

Lewis, R. W. B. *The American Adam.* Chicago: University of Chicago Press, 1955.

Lincoln, Abraham. *Selected Speeches and Writings.* New York: Library of America,
1992.

Lippincott, Benjamin. *Victorian Critics of Democracy.* Minneapolis: University of
Minnesota Press, 1938.

Locke, John. *A Letter concerning Toleration.* Ed. James Tully. Indianapolis: Hackett, 1983.

————. *Two Treatises of Government.* Ed. Peter Laslett. Cambridge: Cambridge
University Press, 1988.

Macedo, Stephen. *Liberal Virtues.* Oxford: Clarendon Press, 1990.

MacIntyre, Alasdair. *After Virtue.* Notre Dame, IN: University of Notre Dame
Press, 1984.

Mander, Jerry, and Edward Goldsmith, eds. *The Case against the Global Economy.*
San Francisco: Sierra Club Books, 1996.

Markowitz, Linda. "Employee Participation at the Workplace." *Critical Sociology*
22, no. 2 (1996): 89–103.

Marks, Barry A., ed. *Mark Twain's Huckleberry Finn.* Boston: D. C. Heath, 1959.

Marx, Karl. *Karl Marx: Selected Writings.* Ed. David McLellan. Oxford: Oxford
University Press, 2000.

McWilliams, John P., Jr. *Political Justice in a Republic.* Berkeley: University of California Press, 1972.

McWilliams, Wilson Carey. *The Idea of Fraternity in America.* Berkeley: University of California Press, 1973.

Mill, John Stuart. *On Liberty and Other Essays.* Ed. John Gray. New York: Oxford University Press, 1991.

Mizener, Arthur. *Twelve Great American Novels.* New York: New American Library, 1967.

Morrison, Toni. *Beloved.* New York: Vintage, 2004.

Nash, Roderick. *Wilderness and the American Mind.* New Haven: Yale University Press, 2001.

Nietzsche, Friedrich. *Beyond Good and Evil.* Trans. by Walter Kaufmann. New York: Random House, 1966.

———. *On the Genealogy of Morality.* Ed. Keith Ansell-Pearson. Trans. Carol Diethe. Cambridge: Cambridge University Press, 1994.

———. *Untimely Meditations.* Trans. R. J. Hollingdale. Cambridge: Cambridge University Press, 1997.

———. *Thus Spoke Zarathustra.* Trans. R. J. Hollingdale. New York: Penguin, 1969.

Nozick, Robert. *Anarchy, State, and Utopia.* New York: Basic Books, 1974.

Nussbaum, Martha. *Love's Knowledge.* New York: Oxford University Press, 1990.

———. *Poetic Justice.* Boston: Beacon Press, 1995.

Okin, Susan M. *Justice, Gender, and the Family.* New York: Basic Books, 1991.

Paine, Thomas. *Common Sense.* New York: Penguin Books, 1986.

Plato. *The Republic.* Trans. Francis MacDonald Cornford. London: Oxford University Press, 1945.

Posner, Richard. *Law and Literature.* Rev. ed. Cambridge: Harvard University Press, 1998.

Pound, Ezra. *Jefferson and/or Mussolini.* New York: Liveright, 1936.

———. *Selected Prose: 1909–1965.* Ed. William Cookson. London: Faber and Faber, 1973.

Powell, Timothy B. *Ruthless Democracy.* Princeton: Princeton University Press, 2000.

Putnam, Robert. *Bowling Alone.* New York: Simon and Schuster, 2000.

Rawls, John. *Political Liberalism.* New York: Columbia University Press, 1996.

———. *A Theory of Justice.* Rev. ed. Cambridge: Harvard University Press, 1999.

Raz, Joseph. *The Morality of Freedom.* Oxford: Clarendon Press, 1986.

Ringe, Donald A. *James Fenimore Cooper.* New York: Twayne Publishers, 1962.

Rosenblum, Nancy. *Another Liberalism.* Cambridge: Harvard University Press, 1987.

Rothkopf, David. "In Praise of Cultural Imperialism?" *Foreign Policy,* Summer 1997, 38–53.

Rousseau, Jean-Jacques. *The Social Contract.* Trans. Christopher Betts. Oxford: Oxford University Press, 1994.

Rowe, John Carlos. *At Emerson's Tomb.* New York: Columbia University Press, 1997.

Sandel, Michael J. *Democracy's Discontent.* Cambridge: Harvard University Press, 1996.

——. *Liberalism and the Limits of Justice.* Cambridge: Cambridge University Press, 1982.

Saxton, Alexander. *The Rise and Fall of the White Republic.* London: Verso, 1990.

Schiller, Friedrich. *Essays.* The German Library, vol. 17. Ed. Walter Hinderer and Daniel O. Dahlstrom. New York: Continuum, 1995.

——. *Schiller's Poems.* Chicago: The Henneberry Company, n.d.

Shepard, Walter J. "Democracy in Transition." *The American Political Science Review* 29, no. 1 (February 1935): 1–20.

Shklar, Judith. *Ordinary Vices.* Cambridge: Harvard University Press, 1984.

Simpson, David. *The Politics of American English, 1776–1850.* New York: Oxford University Press, 1986.

Smith, David Michael. "Workplace Democracy at College of the Mainland." *Peace Review* 12, no. 2 (June 2000): 257–62.

Smith, Henry Nash. *Mark Twain's Fable of Progress.* New Brunswick, NJ: Rutgers University Press, 1964.

Stack, George J. *Nietzsche and Emerson.* Athens: Ohio University Press, 1992.

Stephen, James Fitzjames. *Liberty, Equality, Fraternity.* Ed. Stuart D. Warner. Indianapolis: Liberty Fund, 1993.

Stowe, Harriet Beecher. *Uncle Tom's Cabin.* New York: Penguin, 1981.

Thiele, Leslie Paul. *Friedrich Nietzsche and the Politics of the Soul.* Princeton: Princeton University Press, 1990.

Thoreau, Henry David. *Civil Disobedience and Other Essays.* New York: Dover, 1993.

——. *Walden; or, Life in the Woods.* New York: Dover, 1995.

Tocqueville, Alexis de. *Democracy in America.* Ed. J. P. Mayer. Trans. George Lawrence. New York: HarperPerennial, 1969.

Twain, Mark. *The Adventures of Huckleberry Finn.* New York: Charles L. Webster, 1885.

——. *A Connecticut Yankee in King Arthur's Court.* New York: Bantam Books, 1981.

——. *Life on the Mississippi.* Vol. 9 of *The Writings of Mark Twain.* New York: Harper and Brothers Publishers, 1911.

——. *The Portable Mark Twain.* Ed. Bernard DeVoto. New York: Viking Press, 1968.

Van Doren, Carl. *The American Novel.* New York: The Macmillan Company, 1924.

Veblen, Thorstein. *The Theory of the Leisure Class.* New York: Dover Publications, 1994.

Walzer, Michael. *Spheres of Justice.* New York: Basic Books, 1983.

Weber, Max. *From Max Weber.* Ed. H. H. Gerth and C. Wright Mills. New York: Oxford University Press, 1946.

Weisbuch, Robert. *Atlantic Double-Cross.* Chicago: University of Chicago Press, 1986.

Whitebrook, Maureen. *Real Toads in Imaginary Gardens.* Savage, MD: Rowman and Littlefield, 1995.

Whitman, Walt. *Complete Poetry and Collected Prose.* Ed. Justin Kaplan. New York: Library of America, 1982.

Wickersham, Jay. "Jane Jacobs's Critique of Zoning: From *Euclid* to Portland and Beyond." *Boston College Environmental Affairs Law Review* 28, no. 4 (Summer 2001): 547–63.

Wilding, Michael. *Political Fictions.* London: Routledge and Kegan Paul, 1980.

Will, George F. *Statecraft as Soulcraft.* New York: Simon and Schuster, 1983.

Yeats, William Butler. *The Collected Poems of W. B. Yeats.* New York: The Macmillan Company, 1960.

Zakaria, Fareed. *The Future of Freedom.* New York: W. W. Norton, 2004.

Zuckert, Catherine H. *Natural Right and the American Imagination.* Savage, MD: Rowman and Littlefield, 1990.

Index